# DELIVERANCE:
# THE FINAL RELEASE
# OF THE CHURCH

## By

## Gary Ray

Unless otherwise noted, all Scripture quotations are from KJV, Thomas Nelson

*Cover Design by Austin Haney*

*Artwork by Aaron Stinson*

Printed in the United States of America

First Printing, November 2015

ISBN  978-0-9916077-3-0

Published by

Aaron Publishing

PO Box 1144

Shelbyville, TN 37162

www.aaronpublishing.com

## *Dedication*

I would like to dedicate this book to my family. To my wife Ophelia, who's steadfastness has been a constant source of strength. To my daughters, Tiffany and Valerie, and my son, Dustin, for their love and belief in me. To my mother, Lorayne, who provided the unconditional love only a mother could give. I would not be where I am today without their support and I dedicate this book to them, for the price they paid through my journey of deliverance and my embarkment on deliverance ministry. Without them, this book would not be possible.

## Endorsements

"Gary Ray is my daddy. I would like to say that having known him since I was born gives me a unique viewpoint of his life, his ministry, and his heart for Christ. I witnessed the part of his life controlled by the devil through the power of addiction. During the darkest times he still desired happiness and desired to find freedom and joy again. He was powerless against the power of Satan in his life...or so he thought. God showed up in a powerful way and placed good Christian leaders in his path to do the work of deliverance in his life. He was healed by God but guided on the path by faithful Christian leaders. I think that experience and the hand of God has led him to this point.

His heart is to see the leaders in ministry equipped to guide others down this same path of deliverance he has walked. In the book he says "It is wonderful to realize what has been given to the body of Christ. Let us take it and begin to teach the rest of the body of

Christ how to be free." He also says, "You have to understand that if the work is done, it will be done through you. If it is accomplished, it will be accomplished by you." This book is his answer to these two calls on his own life. I pray this book reaches those it is intended to reach and that God works in a mighty way through it to bring deliverance to the suffering.

Tiffany Gentry
Daughter of Gary Ray

\*\*\*\*\*\*\*\*\*\*\*\*

"Insight is an important factor when dealing with the issues outlined in this book. Rev. Gary Ray has certainly applied insight in revealing the keys to victory in our ongoing battle with the flesh. Terminology has often been a stumbling block when dealing with this subject. So, Gary has taken a unique approach in dealing with these issues using the simplest of terms. I pray that each reader will apply themselves to the task that faces us all; overcoming Satan's *attempt to conquer our flesh.*

*Dr. Johnny Minick*
*Johnny Minick Ministries*

✶✶✶✶✶✶✶✶✶✶✶✶

*"My brother,*

*The book God has placed in your heart is a needful message for this hour. Like never before, the fabric of our culture is ripped apart. This book is an alarm for the church to wake up and man their battle stations and fight! This book also provides the believer the tools in which to fight effectively...not just throw punches, but land punches that will render the enemy whipped! I love it! I am honored to serve with you in His Kingdom. I love you my friend. Keep giving people HEAVEN everywhere you go."*

*Terry Tripp*
*Terry Tripp Ministries*

✶✶✶✶✶✶✶✶✶✶✶✶

"I have long respected the marvelous testimony of Brother Gary Ray, but it is a pleasant surprise to see that he has taken another step moving into serious writing. I have read through his latest book and am thrilled with the progress he has made. His handling of such a serious topic is to be commended. You can differently gain spiritual insight into the workings of our enemy by reading what Gary offers. Satan is indeed a force to be reckoned with and we need all the direction we can get to defeat him, just as our Lord did. We can learn a lot from a careful study of Gary's book. Of course, our victory lies in the power of Jesus Christ. I recommend you add a copy of Gary's book to your library as a constant guide in your daily battle with Satan. It is a must for your collection.

> Dr. Jimmy Rodgers Snow
> Jimmy Snow Ministries/Son
> of Country Music Legendary
> Hank Snow

************

"This book written by Gary Ray is timely and much needed. There has been much emphasis in churches and books written concerning church growth, revival, healing, prosperity, etc...but nowhere near enough on deliverance. There is a tremendous need for deliverance in the body of Christ. Jesus himself ministered deliverance and He said as recorded in Matthew 10:8 "Heal the sick, cleanse the lepers, raise the dead, cast out demons. Freely you have received, freely give." Neither the command or the need for deliverance has changed. This book is balanced, thorough, and not a difficult read. I highly recommend this for all believers as well as those in preaching ministry."

Apostle Jerry A. Roff
Pastor of Firehouse Church


\*\*\*\*\*\*\*\*\*\*\*\*


"Congratulations to our good friend Gary Ray on the release of his new book. Thank you for allowing the Holy Spirit to speak to you through this book.

9

Sadly, there are many who walk through church doors bound and needing deliverance. Karen and I feel this is an on-time word from God to pastors and the church body. Love and prayers to you as you continue to take this life-changing message to a lost and hurting world."

Mark & Karen Poff
New Harvest Ministries

************

"Deliverance: The Final Release of the Church by Gary Ray is A MUST READ for anyone involved with or familiar with deliverance ministry today. Gary's "no-nonsense," "tell-it-like-it-is" approach to this topic exposes some harsh realities of what is wrong with some deliverance ministries today; BUT THERE IS HOPE! True deliverance can be restored to the church and to its people through prayer, fasting and a true understanding of the authority we have over our adversary, the devil. By applying the principles out-line in this book, Christians can be released from their bondage-state. We can live free again!"

Minster James Kody

\*\*\*\*\*\*\*\*\*\*\*\*

"I have had the honor of working alongside of Gary Ray as he has ministered to the broken, the outcast, the people who may never walk into a church, and the ones the church has given up on because they simply don't know what to do. The Bible talks about Jesus setting the captives free, free from everything. Jesus didn't run when the demon possessed showed up and neither has Gary Ray. Through his many years of deliverance ministry, he has seen it all. The drug addict, the sex addict, the demonized, and the oppressed have all been set free through his ministry. This book is a resource for those in ministry who may be facing the same challenges and need answers. Gary has lived it. He's been there and knows how desperately God wants us to confront the enemy and take the authority He's given us over the enemy. We have spent far too *much time fighting each other over stupid small things while people who need the power of God to touch their lives go unattended too. Deliverance isn't pretty. There aren't many who want to get in the fight, but those who are compassionate understand we can't allow people to live this way. Gary Ray has dedicated his life to listening to the Holy Spirit leading him to pray for and minister to these precious souls. The fight is real. The enemy is real. Deliverance is real. Thank you Gary for being real and sharing with us the truth about this subject. Lives are waiting for someone to be real enough to be honest and tell them they can be set free by the power of Jesus Christ. This book is hope to all of us who have felt captive by something. There is freedom and we need to be the ones setting them free through the power of the Holy Ghost and the authority of Jesus Christ.*

*Tiffany Sweeley*
*Tiffany Sweeley Ministries*

# TABLE OF CONTENTS

# Introduction

We find that the Word tells us that immediately after deliverance has taken place a "house" is swept clean. At that point, a person becomes most vulnerable. The enemy leaves from the inside, but those things that caused the compulsion or problem are still there. He just moves from the inside to the outside. In deliverance when we command demonic forces to leave, the Word says in Matthew12:43-45(NKJ) (43):*"When an unclean spirit goes out of a man, he goes through dry places, seeking rest, and finds none. (44) Then he says, 'I will return to my house from which I came.' And when he comes, he finds it empty, swept, and put in order. (45) Then he goes and takes with him seven other spirits more wicked than himself, and they enter and dwell there; and the last state of that man is worse than the first. So shall it also be with this wicked generation."* We want to be more than just a band aid. We want resolutions to the problems. We feel that this book will not only be a solution but also a resolution.

Not only will we teach people how to be delivered, we will direct the ministry of this book more toward Christians to teach them how to see a person delivered. We must show Christians how to stay delivered by teaching them to put Christ into their life. We also need to teach them how to restructure their life so that the demons that were causing the problem in their life no longer have a place. Someone new has been placed inside them. The Word tells us that where God is, sin can't live: *"Whosoever is born of God doth not commit sin; for his seed remaineth in him: and he cannot sin, because he is born of God"* (1 John 3:9).

The intent of this book is to bring revelation and deliverance to people exposing the lies of the enemy and helping them live the life Christ meant them to live. It is not intended to bring notice to or bring glory to Satan and his deceptive tactics in any way. It is simply important to understand his strategic plans in order to defeat him. Deliverance is not a show of Satan's power, but rather an exposing of his lies and a equipping of the believer to bring glory to God's saving power.

# CHAPTER 1

## Deliverance Defined

It is impossible to say that people can't fall away from God. However, we can teach them how to maintain their relationship with Christ. They can begin to realize that the hope of glory, Jesus living in them, can engulf their lives and that with this kind of relationship the enemy will find it difficult to gain entrance back into their lives. We can close up those entrances by replacing God in all of those areas. Then we are able, in that sense, to set up a wall of protection against letting the enemy back inside.

There is a fine line between badgering someone and boldly attacking the enemy. We must know when God has delivered rather than continue to badger the individual. This can border on spiritual abuse, and we must watch out for this. We need to realize that it takes someone with a strong anointing to minister deliverance. We have dealt with it in our ministry, being labeled "crazy," "a little eccentric," and many other things.

We don't want to become "devil chasers

either." We don't want to be looking behind every bush for a demon. This problem exists in some churches. It is assumed that every person that comes through the door could be demon possessed. We do not want to be like that type of church. We should desire to be well balanced. We want to have knowledge of deliverance. There are demonic forces out there in possession of lives and we want to effectively help change them. We know there are churches that can carry deliverance to the extreme. However, the only way to know if there is a demon is to pull up the bush and see what's there.

Another part of a deliverance ministry is that God doesn't show us what's wrong with people so that we can point it out. He shows us what is hindering them from becoming free. This way they can become all that He has intended for them to be. We also look for what we can build upon. We need to concentrate on their strengths, not what's wrong with them. Then we can create in them a new way to live their lives.

We would like to teach the church how to recognize what is going on in people's lives. We want to teach balance in all aspects of deliverance. We want to use this balanced ministry to teach others how to recognize what is tormenting people and to be able to deliver them. Then after the initial deliverance has been done, we want to teach them how to stay delivered and live their lives based on biblical principles—in a life that is a testimony for Christ.

We want them to be effective in their ministries and no longer tormented and stunted in their growth because of old demonic forces. We hope this book touches many lives. Most of what we speak about will be directed to the church because that's where the biggest need is. If we can teach the church, as well as other ministries, how to recognize these demonic forces, we can also teach them how to effectively deliver these troubled lives. They will learn how to identify the demonic forces and to command them to go and know that they are gone. We must teach them how to apply the Word of God to their lives, thus watching them become victorious.

Hopefully, this book will educate men and women on how to work effectively in the deliverance ministry. We hope to target church leaders so that we might educate them in deliverance and to be able to maintain that deliverance.

In the beginning, the greatest witness for this book is my testimony. I felt the Holy Spirit speaking to me, urging me to write a book using the things I learned over a period of years in a deliverance ministry. After years of drug and alcohol abuse, I experienced deliverance in my personal life. Since that time I have been "come at" or "sought out" many times because of what I experienced in my own deliverance. I realize that some churches deny the existence of the demons I have been fighting. Many people will make the statement that a Christian cannot have demonic forces in their life. Yet, most of the deliverances I will write about in this book were of Christians. I am not saying that everyone was, though they said they had an experience with Christ. Some were actively working in churches. That leads me to believe that maybe our thinking could be wrong.

I read a book, *Demons, The Answer* by the late Lester Sumrall. I realized what was wrong with our thinking. Can a Christian be demon possessed? It really, according to Dr. Sumrall, becomes questions such as "what is a Christian?" and "what is the definition of a Christian?" When you start dealing with definitions, you are asking for problems, because there are too many definitions. A person may belong to a certain denominational church and may think he cannot be demon possessed, but that has nothing to do with the problem. I agree with Brother Sumrall. In my ministry, I realize that there is a better word to use than "possessed." Let us use the word "demonized."

Really, the issue is not whether the person is "demonized" or not. The questions we should ask are, "Is this individual hurting? Does he or she need help?" Our responsibility in ministry is never to separate ourselves from people who need help. That particular issue is something that our denomination doesn't agree upon or accept. The issue is if that person needs help, our responsibility is to help them. We must deal with them in relation to their needs rather than their "name tag." How well do we know this? Because we are connected to certain organizations or denominations that limit us from getting the help we need. We know better than that. Our ministry should never be limited. We should always be available for hurting people.

The Bible teaches that the devil never

wanted to get inside of Paul; rather the devil ran from him. Nowhere does the Bible say to be afraid of the devil. I am concerned that over a period of years we have taught people to be afraid of the devil, to fear the devil. The Word tells us: *"For God hath not given us the spirit of fear\* but of power and of love and of a sound mind"* (2 Timothy 1:7).

So we begin to realize that we are not to fear the devil.

## CHAPTER 2

## Dunamis vs. Exousia Power

*Resist the devil and he will flee from you* (James 4:7).

We have the right to make the enemy run; we have the power over him. There is something the church should know. The church has traveled in Dunamis power {dunamis = miraculous power, unusual ability, worker of miracles, a miracle itself, STRONG 1411.} This is the power that reproduces itself. This is the power that we as Christians can utilize against the enemy. And then there is Exousia power {exousia = superhuman, potentate, token of control, delegated influence, authority, STRONG 1849}. I believe that the enemy knows how to utilize this type of power for evil (2 Thessalonians 2:4). People need to learn how the devil will use the authority given to him to get into their lives.

We have the right to take authority over the devil. But we have to remember when playing in his territory that there is a danger of also playing into his hand. We need to be aware of this, and instead of fear, we should be acquiring knowledge and wisdom. Wisdom is the ability to know how to use the knowledge that God has given us. When we are on the devil's territory, we need to be aware of the danger. The devil doesn't care who you are, but when you get in his territory, you are in danger of him working in your life. Those who are working in the deliverance field need to be aware of what can happen when working in his territory.

Many of the cases documented in this book are true. They are people who love Jesus. They are going to church and professing to be "Christians," and they have allowed themselves to come in contact with demonic forces. Later in the book we will go deeper into how this can happen. It could be as simple as unforgiveness, bitterness, hatred, or anger. These are obsessive and addictive natures. These spirits can control and determine what we are doing, despite what God commands.

There are demonic forces in our lives. It doesn't matter if we love Jesus or not, they simply must be dealt with in order to move into the place that we talk and preach about—the purity and holiness of God.

Only God can produce life. Satan can't produce life. He only brings death. There are a lot of things going on in churches, and this is the reason they aren't successful. Momentary revivals are taking place. Understand, these are necessary and people are helped, but not to the extent that we would like to see. We are not reaching people. We are building numbers, not people. We are not seeing them delivered. We are seeing them come to church and leave with the same problems they came with. They are often being tormented by the same demonic forces because the church does not realize the need for deliverance. **You can't be delivered from something unless you are delivered to something**. Only through Christ can we solve these problems.

When we are dealing with the dark side I feel we need to make the church, or the leaders of these ministries, aware that there are terrible things happening to people everywhere. Since I started to write this book, I became aware that things are changing and I feel it is time for these things to be taught. There is an urgency at this time.

The church must be made aware of what's transpiring. The demonic forces that we are seeing now have a tremendous hold on the church. I'm sure I can't expose all that is going on, but I know that I am to expose a part of it.

I don't want people to think that I have all of the answers. I do know that I have a part of the answer. The church that is without spot, blemish, or wrinkle must come forth (Ephesians 5:27). We need to be aware, that it's not whether a person believes a certain way or not, but they simply need help and we are to meet their needs. When they cry for help, we should be able to help them.

Again, I do believe that we have a responsibility to be able to trust in those who are God chosen.

We are not to create division in the church but help bring unity to the body of Christ. When this happens then we can take care of the demonic forces that are at work in a church.

For years we have allowed people to be tormented because of doctrinal differences. In order to expose demonic forces that have a grip on lives, true holiness must be brought back to the church. The main interest should be that people with demonic issues are set free. My desire for this book is to see people set free.

The one thing that amazes me is the simplicity of the things the enemy uses to get into a person's life. The simplest things, that we would never think would trip an individual, are the things the enemy uses. I became aware of this when I saw things happening in my own life and ministry.

My wife and I moved to Brandon, Florida, with a vision to build a ministry. In the process, I saw the hold tradition had on the people that we were pastoring. Some of these people were under demonic control. There were active demonic forces that needed spiritual help.

The traditions that we dealt with were troubling to the Spirit. When I talk about traditions, there are traditions established in the Word of God that we follow. However, I am talking about manmade traditions. I am talking about traditions we have allowed men to decide upon. Even when we knew they were wrong, we wouldn't change them. There were certain demonic activities people were engaging in that the church shouldn't have allowed.

The Word teaches us the following: *"I beseech you therefore, brethren, by the mercies of God, that ye present your bodies a living sacrifice, holy, acceptable unto God, which is your reasonable service (1). And be not conformed to this world: but be ye transformed by the renewing of your mind, that ye may prove what is that good, and acceptable, and perfect, will of God" (2)* (Romans 12:1, 2).

## CHAPTER 3

## Uncovering Demonic Forces
## Within the Church

There was a woman with a Jezebel spirit (Jezebel Spirit is a termagant or false teacher) who had had been teaching some of the women in the church before I got there. So we began to use her to teach. She began to teach not to trust man. We know from the Word, that from the beginning of time, God has chosen men and women as spiritual leaders. This woman was teaching the church not to follow God's chosen.

We had a hard time getting her out of the church. After she left, we thought it was over but she was still controlling the women. When she was at the church we could see what she was doing. When she left, she was on the phone to the women all the time. All we could see at the time was that we needed to get rid of this problem. From this particular situation we realized that we couldn't just run this spirit off, we needed to kill it—not the person but the Jezebel spirit.

29

In the Song of Solomon 2:15 it says: *"Take us the foxes, the little foxes, that spoil the vines; for our vines have tender grapes."*

We need to be aware that at times it's not those big boisterous situations that will destroy the church; it is the little things that are not dealt with that will just keep nibbling away. We were very cautious in dealing with this situation. We could not push the problem aside. We must set these people free, not just run them out of the church. They are under the control of the spirit of witchcraft, and we must get them delivered or they will continue to undermine whatever work that is trying to be accomplished. They must be delivered to get the help they need.

There are many issues we are dealing with here. This Jezebel spirit we are discussing is demonic. I am convinced today the Jezebel spirit is one of the most prevalent spirits in the church. It definitely needs to be dealt with.

While we are looking at the Jezebel spirit, we find it is an unchaste and unclean spirit, intent on the seduction and destruction of ministries. It is the spiritual mafia of the evil underworld. It is assigned to destroy ministries and to make them a laughing stock and ruin their credibility. In the beginning the Jezebel spirit was the spirit of a woman's love of pre-eminence over men. She feels insecure, so must constantly put men down to reinforce her own ego.

There is a lack of understanding of positional places. I believe both men and women have a place in the ministry. Let me clarify this. I believe that God planned a way in terms of how everything should operate. First, men cannot be birthers. Women are the only birthers. Women understand the pain of birthing. I have found most strong intercessors are women because they do understand the process of birthing.

We may wonder how this Jezebel spirit got such a grip on a ministry. One reason could be that men went off to war, and they didn't come back to the church. It was left up to the women to run the church. I think we need men in the church as well as women. I do not want people to get the wrong idea about what I am saying. I believe women have a big part to play in the ministry. Women have always had a big part in my ministry. I became aware, in pastoring, of this Jezebel spirit, and using the discernment that God has given me I was able to deliver many. This Jezebel spirit has had a strong control over many ministries I have been in since. This Jezebel spirit in control of ministries is not of God, but is a spirit of witchcraft.

I feel at times—and I know it is hard to believe—that people can become controlled by this demonic force, thinking all the time it is God. This is why we need to keep ourselves pure and close to God. It is so easy for the enemy to slip in and get a hold of lives. They feel it is of God because Satan is so good at counterfeiting and making people think he is of God. When left alone, this spirit will grow stronger. Before too long, the spirit has full control of the person and that person no longer knows right from wrong—because it has become a way of life.

# CHAPTER 4

## Spiritual Change

I would like to talk about the meetings going on around the country. I would say everything that glitters is not gold. We know that a true move of God is not based on emotion, but brings a definite change to individuals' lives, especially those whom are touched by these meetings. The changes that you can see will last forever. The Word says in Luke 19:10: *"For the Son of man is come to seek and to save that which was lost."*

This is what revival is all about. He came to teach us to go out and reach the lost. This is the great commission Jesus gave to us, and we should make this one of the most important acts in our ministries. This is more important than an emotional move. That is not to say emotion is not a part of it. I have a strong feeling about the emotional things that go on. They are not always true. I don't think emotions should be the main issue. Yes, I have been slain in the spirit and know that it is of God. I have been drunk in the spirit; so drunk that I couldn't

33

stand up. I have danced. I have laughed. I have wept. All of these are things that verify in the natural, what we feel in our spirit.

I want you to know I am not talking against emotion, I am simply saying that if emotion is all that there is, then God didn't get the glory. We can have a rip-roaring service where everybody is emotionally touched in the service, and that is great. There is also a responsibility for ministry to go beyond the emotion. We can emotionally excite people and still not create any spiritual change in their lives. We need to emphasize the spiritual change in a life. If we preach a message without Christ, what good is it? He simply came "to seek and to save that which was lost" and our responsibility is the same. I think we need to emphasize the things that bring stability into lives.

# CHAPTER 5

## Hindrance to Deliverance

Concerning men and women in leadership, they must have integrity, carrying a strong anointing as Jesus did in Luke 4:18: *"The Spirit of the Lord is upon me, <u>because</u>\* He hath anointed me to preach the gospel to the poor; he hath sent me to heal the brokenhearted, to preach deliverance to the captives, and recovering of sight to the blind, to set at liberty them that are bruised."*

The name **Jesus** means the anointed one, and we are to be like him. When we have this anointing and have been taught about demons, and when we see people chasing after these movements, we know how to deal with them. We will not fall victim to them. We will begin to see the people healed. We need to teach those in deliverance ministries how to recognize what is and what is not a move of God. They need to be taught how to recognize demons. We will find what satisfies the flesh will not satisfy the spirit. We must realize there is a lot of work to do in the body of Christ.

\*Underline added at author's discretion.

Remember when the movie *1984* (Big Brother is Watching You) showed a computer that was able to watch what everyone was doing? We are living in this age now. No one is immune. The government knows what is going on in our lives. They are involved in every aspect of our lives. We are no longer in control of our children. We have come to the place where the government is now telling us how to raise our children. We can no longer discipline our children for fear of the government. We are not to abuse children. I believe there are discipline methods that need to be instituted. We now have children's rights. They have some of the same rights that adults have. I'm not saying that children have no rights, but I believe that when a mother or father is taking care of children and raising them properly—feeding, clothing, and seeing to their needs—they should have the right to choose how to teach and discipline their own children.

The Bible instructs us (Proverbs 22:6) that we are to train our children properly. If we train them in this way, the scripture says when they grow old they will not depart from it. So, if children are given their own set of rights, they are not subject to the rights of their parents and biblical principles. We understand then why they are dealing with the problems of today. The Word tells us: *"without a vision, the people perish* (Proverbs 29:18) (KJV). Other interpretations say that when there is no re-evaluation, the people cast off all restraint and they will run wild. Some children are still under the grip of this demonic force. There are ministries who have maintained biblical principles concerning the discipline of the children. They are able to teach others, and we praise God for these ministries.

It was Khrushchev that once said that we will defeat America and never fire the first shot, but will destroy it from within. He knew that if they could destroy the American family, they could destroy America. The family is where the values are. God instituted the family: the father, the mother, and then the children. That's the way it is to be. There should be respect on both sides, but our children need to be taught to respect adult authority. A large majority of young people do not have this respect. It's easy to see the imperfection in others, but not quite as easy to see it in ourselves. There is a possibility that this could be a hindrance in the deliverance ministry.

Deliverance: The Final Release of the Church

# CHAPTER 6

## Prerequisite For Deliverance Ministers

We are finding out in the deliverance ministry that it is important to deal with the imperfections in our lives. Then it will be easier to deliver others. It's easy to see the faults of others and not the faults in ourselves. *"And why beholdest thou the mote that is in thy brother's eye, but considerest not the beam that is in thine own eye?"* (Matthew 7:3). We need to deal with the things in our life in order to effectively minister deliverance to others.

Those who are anointed in the deliverance ministry have the Holy Spirit. This sets them apart and puts them in a position where they can help others in bondage to demonic forces. It is the Holy Spirit which allows them to bring deliverance.

The enemy will use the most innocent things to do the greatest damage to people. We should never be motivated by the same things that motivate the flesh. We need to help people realize that only through Christ do they have the ability to defeat the demonic forces in their lives.

We make a mistake in using past experiences in deliverance. Deliverance must never become mechanical. In past methods of deliverance, demons would scream, holler, and slither on the floor like snakes, trying to spit, throw up, and curse the ones doing the deliverance. This method worked well then. You must understand that God does not always work by the same method and so we must always seek God and operate only in what the Holy Spirit gives us for the lives needing deliverance. What God does for each individual is new and fresh and is created just for them. In deliverance, we should be aware of what the Holy Spirit is saying now and not operate on what we have learned from the past.

I understand that God can use anything He wills to accomplish deliverance in a life. God will only use someone with a strong anointing to administer deliverance. Those in the ministry of deliverance do not wake up one morning and become "devil chasers." Those in a deliverance ministry must be called.

I feel that I was called into the deliverance ministry, that God placed this call on my life, and that there are specific things I am to accomplish in this ministry.

Deliverance should be a part of every ministry. The deliverance ministry does not happen by osmosis—putting an old Bible under your pillow and waking up with all of the answers in the morning—neither does deliverance. Deliverance is something that must be taught by those with the call of deliverance and experience in their life. It takes a strong anointing to minister deliverance. There must be balance between the anointing and learning. Those who are in a deliverance ministry have an obligation to help train others being called into this type of ministry.

It's like discipleship—God wants everybody to be a disciple, but they are not born, they have to be taught. Deliverance is accomplished in the same way. God anoints people to have the power to command demons to come out, and these people need to be taught. There are many issues not being dealt with in today's ministries. These concerns need to be managed if a ministry is to be without spot or wrinkle and manifesting true deliverance. We know it is not in a building; it is in individuals with the call on their life. The Word says in 1 Corinthians 3:16: *"Do you not know that you are the temple of God and that the Spirit of God dwells in you?" And, in 1 Corinthians 6:19: "Or do you not know that your body is the temple of the Holy Spirit who is in you, whom you have from God, and you are not your own?"*

We are His temple and He lives in us. His righteousness in us is the most important thing. This is what we are trying to produce through deliverance. Our desire is for them to manifest His righteousness.

## CHAPTER 7

## Identification:  Natural or Supernatural

We may ask, what are demons? What do they do? If we are to be able to deliver people from them, we must not be ignorant about demons. On page 827 of the *International Standard Bible Encyclopedia* we find that the words 'demon,' 'demonic,' and 'demonology.' Demon is described as an unclean or evil spirit. The word 'demon' seems to originally have two closely related meanings: 1) a deity and a spirit superhuman, but not supernatural in the former sense; and 2) a general reference to vulgarly conceived personal beings akin to men and yet belonging to the unseen realm.

Frequently I will refer to *God's Plan for Man* by Finis Jennings Dake. I like his research, especially lesson 6, page 84, where he begins his study on Satan and the spirit world. We find through study the Bible is the only book in the world giving us any insight into the heavenly realm. There are many books written, but the Bible is the one book that gives us direct insight that we can trust. This does not discredit books written about demons. Still, the greatest record we have is the Bible. There are scriptures revealing what we need to know about this unseen world. There are many demonic spirits in this world and they are revealed in scripture. There are many different demonic spirits that we find in the unseen world or the underworld of departed spirits, and even those invisible things about us on the earth.

There is a supernatural and natural world, and there is a very thin line that separates these two worlds. This is why it's so easy for the enemy to get into our lives. I have always known about the familiar spirits that he operates through. For instance, if you have had an alcohol problem, Satan will try to trip you up with alcohol because he knows this is the easiest way to get you. In the same respect if you, however, ever had a drug problem, he's going to put every "Old Druggie" you were involved with in your path, hoping to draw you back into drugs.

Demons are real—when we look in the Bible we find that the subject of demons is spoken of frequently. The word "demon" itself is not found in scripture, but we know it to mean evil spirit or devil. The word "devil" is used to describe Satan, the ruler of demons, and we find this in Matthew 9:30: *"But the Pharisee said he casteth out devils through the prince of devils."*

We know Satan to be the chief evil spirit and the original source of all evil in this world. We can see his handiwork. In *God's Plan for Man* where we find the Greek word for 'devil' used in connection with Satan, this word is 'diabolos.' The meaning is adversary, false accuser, slanderer, or devil. It is used of men in 1 Timothy 3:11, 2 Timothy 3:3, and Titus 3:3. It was also applied to Judas, when he became an adversary of Christ, in John 6:70: *"Jesus answered them, Have not I chosen you twelve, and one of you is a devil?"*

There are 34 Bible references where Satan is called the chief adversary of God, and Satan is translated as "devil." In another 76 places, both words 'devil' and 'devils' are found. Evil spirits, or demons, are derived from two different Greek words: 1) daimon and 2) daimonion. They both translate to "evil spirit" or "devil." There is only one devil, but there are many demons or little imps to do his work.

The devil has an angelic body, and we must remember at the time of his fall he was the most beautiful angel in heaven. He has never been the little red man with horns and a pitch fork. I have often thought his beauty was one way in which he was able to deceive so many. We also understand he cannot enter into anyone. Demons who are disembodied spirits can only operate in the material world through the possession of men and beasts; they must have a human body to operate through.

I am a firm believer that most demon spirits have a specific characteristic or assignment. There is a demon spirit for every sickness, unholy trait, in all living forms of corruption, every doctrinal error known among men; they have to be cast out in order for that individual to get relief. Traffic with demon spirits is forbidden in the Bible, both Old and New Testaments.

Some churches have taken out of their doctrinal teachings those things that make them uncomfortable or afraid. This is said in a broad sense. Not all churches want to deal with demonic forces. There was a time several years ago I was invited to a church and was talking with the pastor. He knew of my ministry and said he didn't want me coming in and causing any spirits to throw up on his new carpet. Not everyone wants to deal with demonic forces. If you find a church that does, please know first that the church really needs to understand how to accomplish this task. Demons cannot be defeated by avoidance and lack of understanding of how they operate. We must understand 2 Corinthians 2:11: *"Lest Satan should get an advantage of us; for we are not ignorant of his devices."*

We must become aware of the problem that arises when we begin to deal with demons. There is no need to be afraid. We are God's chosen people; we know through the word that we have power over Satan. We know what James 4:7 says: *"Submit yourselves therefore to God. Resist the devil, and he will flee from you."*

We know demonic forces are to flee upon command, but sometimes there are areas in our lives we have trouble in claiming victory. There may be those Christians who have not learned how to truly submit themselves to God. The ability to deliver people belongs to the body of Christ. There is also a need to be teaching others on how to deal with demons.

There are many people sitting with demonic forces in their lives who are unable to let go. It could be the spirit of perversion, or something as ordinary as prescription drugs. We know many in society are hooked on different types of medication. This will not be a popular statement—I believe the secular system is destroying people by over medicating them. Only God, not the system, can deliver a person.

One of the problems plaguing young people today is the attention deficit syndrome, and the world is putting them on drugs. Some of these young people, not all, need spiritual help and possibly deliverance. We know we have a prescription drug problem in this country. We should not take these problems for granted. Over 50% of the world is plagued with some kind of mental problem, from depression to stress. Could these be demonic? We may need to address this problem, instead of just giving prescription drugs.

We like to talk about marijuana, cocaine, crack cocaine, meth, and heroin. These are problem drugs and there are others. I can certainly talk about drugs, because in March of 1980 I was in serious trouble as a cocaine addict with a habit costing $1,500 to $2,000 dollars a week. Being a part of the music industry, leasing and driving buses and working with many major groups, it was so easy to become a drug addict. Being on the drugs put me on an emotional roller coaster. These problems certainly need to be addressed. They are, without a doubt, demonic in their origin.

Deliverance:  The Final Release of the Church

## CHAPTER 8

## Authority of the Believer

*(17) And these things follow those who believe, <u>in my name</u>\* they will cast out demons; they will speak with new tongues; (18) And they will take up serpents; and if they drink anything deadly, it will by no means hurt them; they will lay hands on the sick and they will recover.*

Mark 16:17, 18 (NKJ TRANSLATION)

Authority to deliver people is given to the believer, and we need to be exercising it. Are we hoping things will get better and straighten out, that people will get better? There are certain things we must do ourselves. The writer of the scripture says that these things will follow those who believe. "In my name <u>they</u> will" not I will, or God will, but <u>they</u> will cast out demons. Who are "they?" "They" are the believers. God spoke into my spirit putting this book together. There is a need for us to realize who we are in Christ. My prayer is this will be a readable book; one that will offer solutions.

\*Underline added at the author's discretion.

One thing God has put into my spirit is how the body can be attacked by a virus that will grow—being unaware it is there until it is full grown. The flu virus can be in a human body up to ten years before it manifests itself fully grown. Just like the terrible plague of AIDS, it can be in your body growing for a long time before it manifests itself. Like these things in the natural body, there may be a virus in the body of Christ.

Numerous Christians have taken so many scriptures out of context and used them to make people think that just by saying a few words, everything is okay. Yet, roots of anger, bitterness, and unforgiveness are still growing within us like a virus. Let me ask, "How can we be considered pure if these things are hidden in our lives?"

A delivered mind will create a new direction in a person's life. The scripture tells us that when deliverance happens, we become a new creation. All things become new, and old things pass away. Do you think it is time for deliverance to come back to the body of Christ?

*"Therefore if any man be in Christ, he is a*

*new creature: old things are passed away; behold, all things are become new"* (2 Corinthians 5:17 (NKJ)).

Other scriptures that will become very important to us are:

*"The Spirit of the Lord is upon me, because he hath anointed me to preach the gospel to the poor; he hath sent me to heal the brokenhearted, to preach deliverance to the captives, and recovering of sight to the blind, to set at liberty them that are bruised"* (Luke 4:18).

*"The spirit of the Lord God is upon me; because the Lord hath anointed me to preach good tidings unto the meek; he hath sent me to bind up the brokenhearted, to proclaim liberty to the captives, and the opening of the prison to them that are bound"* (Isaiah 61:1).

We see that the word 'me' is in the New and Old Testaments. It is important for those who are called into a deliverance ministry to become acquainted with this type of ministry. It is also important to have a strong prayer life. Everything in a deliverance ministry is not mechanical. We realize some of the things we will need for a successful deliverance ministry will only come through prayer and fasting. We need those in the body of Christ who are preparing for a deliverance ministry to realize the need to seek God to receive this special anointing so they can help get people delivered. For the spirit of the Lord is upon 'me;' you who are called into this ministry are the ones who are going to cause things to happen. We want those who are called to reach the place where they can operate and do the things that God wants them to.

There are those people who are in established religions and denominations who really do not want deliverance to take place. I sure don't want to put everyone in this box. There are so many who have seen the deliverance ministry abused and this is why they shy away from it. They want people to be set free and to understand their God-given rights for deliverance. Their true desire is for them to come into a complete knowledge of Jesus Christ. They want them to realize the power and authority that comes with a true anointed deliverance ministry. They want them to know those who are truly called and anointed in the deliverance ministry. There are some in denominations that have felt the need to keep the people in the dark. This has happened time after time in certain ministries because those in charge didn't want people to gain too much knowledge—if they do, then they can't be controlled and held in line. I strongly disagree with this.

I believe that when people are truly delivered they are set free. They are then able to become workers in the ministry. I don't believe for a minute an individual is brought into a ministry merely to warm a pew and give their tithes (understand that tithing is still a commandment).

Everyone has a ministry calling that they are supposed to be fulfilling. The Word says in Ephesians 4:16 (KJV): *"From whom the whole body fitly joined together and compacted by that which every joint supplieth, according to the effectual working in the measure of every part, maketh increase of the body unto the edifying of itself in love."*

We realize how important it is for the body of believers to come together. The Word tells us to assemble together. The unity of the early worshipers, not their ability to lay hands on the sick, or raise the dead or cast out demons, was the greatest church builder. It was their ability to show love for one another—this was their finest building tool. I am a firm believer the true liberty we read about in Luke 4:18 and Isaiah 61:1 can't happen until we become aware of deliverance and realize through this anointing we are able to set people free. With all the excess baggage that is hanging on to people's lives today, they cannot motivate and operate freely. Deliverance has to come back to the body of Christ, and those who are in charge must realize when people are truly set free, they will not run, but will stay where God has put them. I believe that when people are totally set free it is then easier for them to channel their actions in a spiritual direction and they will become more beneficial to the body of Christ.

Deliverance will not create anarchy in the church. True discipleship in the body of Christ can lead to the place of true power and authority. I am talking about exousia power, as mentioned earlier. This power is going to manifest itself when you say the words, "In the name of Jesus, I command that demonic force to come out!" You know it is going to happen because of the authority of His Word.

Deliverance in anyone's life will take the enemy out of control and put God in control of their life; giving them a greater insight into what God wants for them. Our greatest desire is to see all who are in darkness brought into his marvelous light.

If we go back and simply take a look at the history of the "spirit filled" movement with Smith Wigglesworth of the Azusa Street Movement, we find there was a freedom to move when the spirit moved. When the spirit moved, people were delivered and received many miracles. When men saw these things happen and realized they were not in control of this move of God, the men who were in charge began to remove those things that made them uncomfortable so they could maintain control. Pentecostal denominations were also guilty of some of the same practices. My position is they were not wrong in their inception, but over a period of years we see it not as a spirit-led movement, but a denomination of men controlling people. Deliverance breaks the bondage of control in people's lives, liberates them, and sets them free. We are in a time where a spirit of deliverance is being given back to the church that sets people free and puts them in a position where the Holy Spirit can be in leadership of their life.

# CHAPTER 9

## Dealing with Familiar Spirits

Familiar spirits are able to attach themselves to people's lives, and we don't even
recognize that we have a problem—we
don't realize we have a need for deliverance. We don't realize that a familiar spirit
has attached itself. This is not true in every
case, because those who have a smoking
problem are aware that they are smoking.
Cigarettes are an addiction, just like Cokes
and coffee. All of these things are very addictive, yet not all of them are demonic. I
don't believe people realize how easy it is
for some these to become demonic.

There are familiar spirits we accept back in
our lives. When people need help and then
all of a sudden refuse help, that lets those in
deliverance know that a familiar spirit has
been able to attach itself again. (**AND WE
WONDER IF THEY WERE EVER DE-
LIVERED IN THE FIRST PLACE.**)
Psychiatry, psychology, and what people
have learned concerning the mind have become huge obstacles in the process of getting people truly delivered. I'm sure that

the feathers of some of my friends in the field are going to be ruffled by these statements. We know there are men and women working in the system who are concerned and truly want to help people. We must realize the system is not going to do anything to set people free. The government wants to keep control over people, and we are discovering medication is a good way to accomplish this goal.

I have been very cautious about regression therapy because there is always the ability to plant thoughts in the minds of patients that are not really there. I believe sometimes we can go back through a person's past and find out things. Probing the memory is serious, and we must be very careful to make sure we are not playing with people's emotions. As a deliverance minister, who spends quite a bit of time with people in distress, I am very cautious not to create things in their minds. There is no need to impress people. I am truly in this ministry to see people totally set free. I do believe that there have been many seeds planted in people's minds which have caused them to believe things have happened in their life which are not true. There are people who have problems from their past, and we must recognize the real problem and seize the opportunity to remove the demonic force from their lives.

There are those in trouble from their past who are in need of help but because of media attention, mind problems become bigger. One of the greatest hindrances is the knowledge that has surfaced concerning the mind and how people act or react. This is a huge obstacle for those who are given the anointing of deliverance. We must learn to defeat this "mind" syndrome happening in the world today.

It will be hard to put into book form what the church has denied being in existence for years. Demonic forces allowed to stay in the church were able to become comfortable and gain strength. Believe it or not, the demonic forces in the church have not diminished, but have grown stronger. The longer we allow them to be there, the stronger they will become. They are not going to come out or be driven out easily. They are not going to give up the ground they have been able to acquire over the years. I believe the church needs to be taught how to deliver people again. I believe the leaders in some churches will not be receptive of the deliverance theory because it will cause them to lose the control that they've had for years. It may cause some to lose big ministries. When deliverance is taught, we will see true men of God come to the forefront. We are beginning to see this happening.

I believe deliverance is a method that God will use to bring the church back to its rightful place with Him. We need to look at certain aspects of the deliverance ministry and realize spiritual warfare is an intricate part of this ministry. It could be where we have been missing it. Because without the knowledge of how to fight spiritually after the person has been delivered, the familiar spirits will come back again. After deliverance a teaching program needs to be put into effect in order to instruct people on how to maintain their deliverance.

A program needs to be initiated in all ministries to make sure that people are taught to live problem free. Not every church will be able to maintain a 12-step program for those addicted to drugs or alcohol. A curriculum can be initiated with skilled instructors who can contact the students and follow up with them.

A training manual needs to be developed—we are trying to accomplish this task with this book. People who work in this area need to be anointed for this work, being able to give individuals scriptures that will give them strength, helping to encourage them to continue to grow in the Word. There needs to be a study book, and each person being delivered must go through this program and graduate. Then they will be strong enough to recognize and deal with familiar spirits who will return to them again.

When we look at an alcoholic, we realize he lives in an alcoholic environment, either at work or drinking with friends. So, after he is delivered and becomes a part of the church, he has to go back into the same environment. There must be a program available to teach them how to disconnect from the world and begin to rely on spiritual help from God to get through.

The spirits that attach to people, drugs, alcohol, tobacco, sexual perversion, and even homosexuality are entrances that the devil will use to get back in their lives. The scripture tells us that when a house is swept clean, it is at its most vulnerable state.

Those demonic forces that have been delivered out of an individual will come back and bring seven more even worse than the ones which just left.

*"When the unclean spirit is gone out of a man, he walketh through dry places, seeking rest; and finding none, he saith, I will return unto my house whence I came out. And when he cometh, he findeth it swept and garnished. Then goeth he, and taketh to him seven other spirits more wicked than himself; and they enter in, and dwell there; and the last state of that man is worse than the first"* (Luke 11: 24-26).

These demonic forces that have been delivered will come back unless Godly things are placed in the house—I am speaking of spiritual furniture. When a person is delivered, the very first thing there needs to be is a discipleship program to teach them how to fight those spirits that will return to their life.

This is hard to talk about, since it deals with my own deliverance. Realize that deliverance is a process of moving into a new position of spirituality. It is important to know God is giving this back to the church, and it will be a hard message for people to accept. We know this process has to happen. I have experienced tremendous growth in the spiritual realm of understanding and reasoning. It could never happened—had deliverance not come to me. No one came to me as I am doing now and told me that I needed to deal with the demonic forces controlling my life. Yet, someone did see things in me as my ministry grew and was able to deal with them. I thank God every day for those who came to me and cared enough to speak to me about these things. I go back, from time to time, to the first revival I held after becoming a full-time evangelist. I saw a great move of God for someone so young in the ministry. I learned a lot being new to the full gospel movement. I had just been filled with the Holy Ghost, just a very short time. I saw many great things happen during this revival. People were touched in many mighty ways. I had never experienced such events before in my life. I never will forget the things I saw in those meetings.

It was a very small building, and the pews were very close to the platform, and the altar was very small. We were laying hands on people and seeing them fall to the floor. We were amazed that they never bumped their heads on the pews. It seemed as though their heads would, literally, go through the benches—their heads and body parts would be lying under the bench. The only way they were able to get there was by the mighty power of God. It was one of the miracles that God brought to pass.

The second or third week into the revival the pastor and his wife asked if they could talk with me in one of the Sunday school rooms before the service. I followed them to the back room and the pastor told me that he had seen something that bothered him. He said it could eventually destroy my ministry and he proceeded to explain. As the pastor watched the people he could see in the spirit realm that if he put his hands in front of their eyes, their attention still would only be on me. He said that God began to show him the one thing able to destroy my ministry was vanity. He realized the people's eyes were fixed on me. He shared how he felt the enemy could use this trick to deceive me into thinking these things were happening because of me. His wife approached me and pretended to break an egg over my head while saying, "I am going to allow the Holy Spirit to fall over you, to free you, from this enemy that could destroy you and your ministry."

I never will forget the feeling that I had at that moment, as the pastor and his wife delivered me from one of the possibilities that could have destroy my ministry– **"VANITY."** I was aware of what they were saying. I knew vanity and pride could be a fast destroyer of any ministry. I thank God every day that this enemy was stopped before it could go any further. Thank God for those who realize and will take it upon themselves to see deliverance before destruction in an individual's life. I'm not sure some people have not let things slide because of that pride and vanity. Some that could have had great ministries and could have done great things for God have been destroyed and have fallen by these same things. Here is a hard statement to make— Many "church" people are the only ones who don't bury their dead and don't help their wounded; we just leave their carcasses along the roadside of life. It is time for us to realize all have fallen short of the glory of God and made mistakes, allowing familiar spirits back, and they need to be restored.

The word "restore" means to bring back from its original state; in biblical terms this means to make it better than originally. "Old things pass away, **all** things become new." We need this to happen in the church, rather than having to **"come clean."** We have allowed sin to be in the ministries we have entrusted our lives to. There is no purity or holiness in these ministries.

In Toronto, Canada, a pastor, her associate, and I sat in her living room and began to deal with issues in our lives as directed by the Holy Spirit. There were things in my life and theirs we cast out. It was an awesome day of refreshing. This should take place in the body of Christ. We need to understand the importance of a deliverance ministry, which is so crucial at this time. I am not writing this book to impress people, but hopefully to get the church to understand and realize that getting people saved is the most important step—but please don't stop there. We must also get people delivered. I may be crucified for my next statement. Some of the church will deny that a "Christian can be demonized."

But how many are willing to admit that anger, hatred, bitterness, unforgiveness, and resentment are demon forces that many Christians are dealing with today? This is not oppression. If a person loves Jesus, I don't believe the spirit can be demonized, but I believe the physical body can, so demonic spirits are still controlling lives. These spirits can manifest themselves in many ways like: temper, headaches, depression, fatigue, smoking, as well as use of alcohol and drugs. We must deliver them and teach them how to perform spiritual warfare against spirits who will come against them.

## CHAPTER 10

## Temple Maintenance

Being delivered is great, but we must understand how to maintain this deliverance. We must teach that the enemy is a daily attacker of those who love Jesus because we are his prey. Those who are in the "world" are not his prey, he already has them—the alcoholic, the drug addict, the prostitute, etc.—he has them already. It is God's kingdom he wants to destroy. It is the temple he wants to inhabit. Since the beginning, his desire has been to exalt his throne above God's. The only way he can accomplish this is to "taint" those who belong to God. His desire is to seek whom he may kill, steal, or destroy daily—to gain a hold on anyone who loves Christ. I believe that familiar spirits are one form of attack. This is not to say that he will not use other methods; he will use whatever was the biggest problem in your past. Satan will come at you again and again, trying to win you back into his kingdom.

Let's be clear, Satan does not want to physically kill you, if so you would be no further use to him. He wants to steal your job, your joy, and your knowing that the joy of the Lord is your strength. He would love to kill your witness and destroy your ability to operate in spiritual areas. He wants to kill, steal, and destroy you spiritually, so you are no longer working for God. Eventually, when he has used you up, he will definitely kill your physical body by a demonic force such as sickness or some type of disease. Be aware the sickness most likely is a demonic force.

*"For God hath not given us the spirit of fear, but of power and of love and of a sound mind"* (2 Timothy 1:7).

We need temple maintenance, so we know how to keep what we received from God. He (God) said we must renew our mind daily. There must be a daily sanctification. We know there is sanctification that is part of the second work of grace. This sanctification forgives us for our past sins. Then there is a daily sanctification of a renewing of the mind.

*"And be not conformed to this world: but be ye transformed by the renewing of your*

*mind, that ye may prove what is that good, and acceptable, and perfect, will of God"* (Romans 12:2).

In the Old Testament we see Joshua given the position of the second prophetic leader of the nation of Israel. Remember, these are God's people that he brought out from the land of Egypt; out of the very jaws of hell; out of total slavery and took them into the wilderness. Yes, we must understand that it took them 40 years to learn; but at the end, when the young ones were ready to go into the promised land (and there is no doubt in my mind that they were God's people and Joshua was the one given directions to take over), the first thing he said to them was, let us sanctify ourselves holy before the Lord. Let us prepare ourselves. Let us make ourselves ready. Let's prepare ourselves so we will be able to accomplish God's work. It is important to understand we need to renew ourselves daily before the Lord. This is one of the most important parts of temple maintenance.

I have come to realize that we cannot survive the problems we are dealing with in society today with the people who caused these problems to start with. How can we solve current societal troubles unless we deal with the psychologists, psychiatrists, educators, and motivators who helped originate most of these problems? How can we call them in to solve problems they helped create with their liberal thinking, being promoted throughout society? When you can create a question in some minds about the very existence of God, and his ability to give them a better life, then it is easy to justify sin and immorality.

There have been enough questions about what level we are to serve God on, or what level of commitment we are willing to give God. I would simply say this, **"We must be willing to die for Him."**

The scriptures tell us that we are to take up the cross and follow Christ.

*"Then Jesus beholding him loved him, and said unto him, One thing thou lackest: go thy way, sell whatsoever thou hast, and give to the poor, and thou shalt have treasure in heaven: and come, take up the cross, and follow me."* (Mark 10:21)

If then we are to take up the cross, we must come through the same process He asked them to come through. No, not to die and live again physically, but spiritually, by crucifying sin in our lives and coming to Him with a willingness to die in every area of our lives spiritually.

*"Having therefore these promises, dearly beloved, let us cleanse ourselves from all filthiness of the flesh and spirit perfecting holiness in the fear of God"* (2 Corinthians 7:1).

This is the only way it will work. There are those who do not want true deliverance because it will bring repentance. When deliverance comes to the body of Christ, revival is just around the corner. We know there are those who need repentance and need to return to God. There are some, but not all, churches that have been involved in emotionalism. There has not been a sincere change in their lives. Many have no motivation to go beyond what they can feel in the physical. The body of Christ needs true repentance and true deliverance. People need to move beyond the emotional/feel good state, to the spiritual. When true deliverance arrives, we become spiritual men.

Change may not come easily. It may hurt, but we are talking about what will transform lives.

# CHAPTER 11

## Understanding Demonic Forces

There is a movement in ministries today that mimics deliverance. People who have come through this type of deliverance appear to be putting more in than they are taking out. This can be a satanic move or a new age move, whatever you wish to call it. Though people think they are being delivered, they are being filled with demonic forces. We need to be aware of witches and warlocks who love to visit churches where they can do most of their major work. There has to be a true deliverance from this, and it comes through true repentance. The person must repent to be delivered. Many people will accept deliverance, but not true repentance.

We are bombarded daily by the new age movement. Many organizations we associate with, being Christians, are nothing more than new age. It was not God's plan to have an animal's life become more important than a human life. God put men in control. If you look at Adam, you know he was given dominion over the animals. We have the same dominion today. We should never mistreat or abuse animals. We have organizations such as Greenpeace and Sierra Club that, in my opinion, are new age organizations. There is the possibility if you kill an animal you can serve more prison time than for taking a human life. You can also see in the inner cities where gangs are running rampant. You know animals mark their territory; if you look at the gangs today, you realize when you see walls and buildings with their signature on it, they are marking their territory. Here is something for us to think about—could it be the spirit of bestiality?

In fighting demonic forces, sometimes our mind sees a demon with fangs dripping blood and bloodshot eyes, snarling like a dog. We must remember that Lucifer was an angel of light, and he was not a red man with horns and pointed tail carrying a pitch fork. Flip Wilson started the saying (and it has even been said in the pulpit), **"The devil made me do it."** The devil never makes you do it. We do sinful things because we want to do them or are addicted to them. The answer to this is **(IT IS SIN)**.

One of the ways the enemy comes to us is

as an angel of light. We need to be honest. For instance, when a man sees a pretty lady in a small bathing suit, that is not ugly, but it is a means for the enemy to destroy a marriage and two lives—the young woman and the man that lusts after her. Chocoholics make up a large percentage of the world. There is nothing more beautiful than a large chocolate cake with thick creamy icing. But, after a large portion of the cake has been consumed, we suffer the sin of gluttony and have truly hurt no one but ourselves. It can be an attitude, it looks so good, but yet it is a demonic force. Just remember as I said earlier, not all demons are red imps with pitchforks.

In regard to racism, there will never be racial equality in America. Our land cannot be healed by segregationists. It will not be healed by political measures. The only way to have racial equality is with a deliverance and a healing in the church concerning racial differences. That issue has never been addressed. I feel that all races have problems. We need to understand that we are talking about racial equalities on all sides. We need to understand that whites are not the racists in every instance. We need to understand that African Americans, Latino Americans, Native Americans, Asian Americans, Americans, and any other pure or racial mixture, need to be healed of their racist feelings against whites and likewise, healing for the whites against all nonwhite races. In parts of the world, it is hatred among people of the same race, but they are of different religious sects. Each race has to be healed of their emotional feelings toward other races.

This could be compared to marriage counseling that I have done. When I talk to the man, I promise you that he is going to tell me everything that is "wrong" in the marriage is the woman's fault. She, in turn, is going to tell me what's "wrong" with him. There has never been a marital issue where there weren't problems on both sides. IF we heal the man's problems, there will still be problems in the marriage. If we heal all the problems in the woman, there will still be troubles in the marriage. There must be healing on both sides. It's the same with different races—there needs to be deliverance on all sides. Some racial problems can be demonic. The enemy wants to keep division so he can divide and conquer. If you can divide a mother and father, you can destroy the family. If you can divide a pastor and his church, you destroy that ministry. If you can divide the races, you will destroy the nation. This is what this response is intended to do. These issues need to be addressed and we need to realize the problem is with us all, and we need to come to terms with that.

One thing I find fascinating is that back in the old days, demons seemed to get more attention than God, when they were allowed to speak, spit, and become physical. They became glorified in some ministries. Today we find a more subtle demonic force at work. They have become more accepted and are able to become a part of a ministry. This is where we have come to. Things that would never have been accepted five years ago are now a normal part of some ministries. The demonic forces in these ministries need to be managed, so we can then deal with deliverance outside of the church. We don't want to become callous to things inside the church. We must handle those things inside the body of Christ before we can handle things outside. It can't be a matter of "physician, heal thyself." The church is where it must happen first.

There is a force that has come through the church recently. It can be called shamanism or voodooism. And it is in the charismatic movement—the laughing movement that is going across the country. I don't want to discredit the spirit of joy or laughter; you have probably experienced it, I have experienced it. The laughing movement has come into mainstream religion. One woman that was interviewed on television some time ago said it's like someone told a good dirty joke! So you can see where anything that makes you feel good is now accepted into the church and made a part of it. There is no discernment today concerning what is God and what is Satan. One goal in writing this book is to show what is happening in some churches. We want to show people how they can deal with the demonic forces in the world. There is a need for us to deal with the demonic forces controlling ministries today. First things first in plain language—the deliverance must start at the head.

I see the breakup of the established church as we know it. We see it happening today with **"The Seeker Sensitive, The Emerging church, and also The Reductionist."** There is a time coming when a more liberal religious movement will come forth and people will not hear sound doctoring. My prayer is that old traditions will come back with a refreshing and renewed move of the spirit. We will see this change in many ministries and they are beginning now. What is coming forth is not an independent ministry. Please understand that there is nothing wrong in established denominations. I believe that ministries need to band together for their needs, strengths, fellowship, and unity. I see a denomination with less control but giving more control back to the individual church—where it can't be hampered by a few men—where men are able to minister freely to the needs of the people.

I believe the seven most frequent words to be used at judgment will be, **"But we never did it that way before."** We see a time coming where there will be a greater freedom to move in the spirit and men will not have any control. We see some ministries where Satan seems to have more control than God. We see ministries that are satisfied with emotionalism and being turned on by laughter with jerking, going into trances, etc. Many are fooled into believing these things are of God rather than recognizing when someone comes through with a true anointing of the Holy Spirit delivering a strong word.

This will always bring direction, correction, and reproof. We see the manifestation of this by the lives of people being changed and seeing them eager to move with God. It has to become a major desire of leaders in ministries to know it is not wrong to correct individual's lives. I'm talking about a true anointing of the Holy Spirit delivered with strong word. Strong word will always bring real change in lives. We can see the manifestation of this when they become eager to move with God. Emotional release will not create change in lives, it is only a momentary high and will not bring a permanent change. I have always said, **"I am not interested in how a high a person can jump or how fast he can run, but I am concerned about the direction he goes when he hits the ground."** This is one of the things we need to be aware of. The only thing that brings change in a life is a strong operation of God's Word. The devil has sowed so much deception in ministries today that deliverance will come from a generation of young converts. Dramatic changes will first come in order for God to be able to move supernaturally through his body.

# CHAPTER 12

## Satan's Plan For Power

There is one type of deliverance needed in the body of true believers of Christ at this time. There needs to be a change of their minds and hearts, so they become open to growth and change as well as a greater acceptance of God's Word. There's much revelation in the world today, yet there is still the need for strong words coming from men who are not willing to compromise God's Word. We must realize God is a God of mercy, had it not been for His mercy we would have been in trouble.

We must come to the realization of our need to accept the depth of God's Word. Another part of deliverance is the demonic forces that have been allowed to continue to be a part of Christian's lives. This has created an instability in many lives; the people become unpredictable and unable to trust in the truth of Christ. It is disturbing when Christians become unstable. In four years of pastoring, we dealt with people who had been in church all of their lives, and because there was no deliverance in the ministries they came from, they were dealing with the same problems all of their lives. When they came to our ministry, they were unstable, and you could not depend on them. When there are demonic forces deeply embedded in their lives it will create unstable Christians. The simplest things, such as anger, bitterness, and unforgiveness can create a nonfunctioning Christian. They are so busy gossiping, back biting, and putting down others that they destroy ministers as well as ministries. We need to realize that these actions create unstable Christians who are unable to make sound spiritual decisions. Their decisions are made in the flesh or with a carnal thinking, not with a spiritual mind. The biggest problem with ministries today is that they are filled with unstable Christians and therefore are unable to maintain sound spiritual direction. It shows in the way they operate. We need to deal with these issues and face them head on.

I am not the only person who knows this. And I am not the only person given this anointing. I have read many pieces by writers who have written about demonic forces. I know without question that these men know how to deal with demonic issues— men like Roberts Liardon. You will find, as we continue, many cases we document are of people who loved Jesus but allowed themselves to encounter demonic forces. In their lives, these forces became addictive, causing them to follow the addictions rather than God. These forces must be dealt with if we are to have purity and holiness.

In prior times, the Holy Spirit revealed some things regarding demonic activity that I had forgotten over the years. I have noticed that demonic activity is more subtle today than what I encountered early on in my ministry. In the beginning when I would be ministering to individuals needing deliverance, we saw the demons cause people to exhibit behavior such as slithering on the floor, puking, and foaming at the mouth. We have heard them snarl, growl, and say blasphemous things before coming out of the person. We have also seen individuals taking the demons back after they had just been delivered. As a result, in the deliverance meetings in which this exorcism occurred, the person who allowed the re-entry continued to engage in ungodly behavior after deliverance. There needs to be more awareness and training for ministries in order for them to be able to recognize these subtle forces and to be able to keep the demonic forces from re-entering these lives.

We have records indicating that deliverance ministries were more prevalent in the days of evangelists such as A.A. Allen, William Branham, and the big tent ministries of Oral Roberts, Jack Cole, and W.V. Grant. When these ministries were operating, there was a greater attempt at deliverance than there has been in later years. Religion became a mainstream business. I am not saying every church or ministry is a business. It is okay for churches to make money, for God wants them to prosper. The Word even indicates that the wealth of the wicked is laid up for the righteous.

*"Evil pursueth sinners; but to the righteous good shall be repayed." "A good man leaveth an inheritance to his children's children; and the wealth of the sinner is laid up for the just"** (Proverbs 13:21-22).

*"And Judah also shall fight at Jerusalem; and the wealth of all the heathen round about shall be gathered together, gold, and silver, and apparel, in great abundance"* (Zechariah 14:14).

The Word backs the fact that the church has great potential. It is not wrong to use finances to bring about desired accomplish-

*Underline added at the author's discretion.

ments in ministry. We are not securing these finances for our personal use, but we realize we can achieve our goals in deliverance ministry. We believe that people are ignorant of deliverance ministries and what could be accomplished through them.

Over the years we have seen the vulgarity of the enemy; he loves to desecrate any ministry, along with the purity and holiness of God. Satan's intent is to desecrate and make those things purely defiled. Holy becomes unholy; this is Satan's desire. We need to be aware of what he is doing in individual's lives. When the church was in the dark ages, still trying to operate as it had for years, the enemy was modernizing. We should have been using television and radio to preach the message of deliverance to the world, instead of calling it the **"devil's tool."** The devil was saying OK, it's my tool and I'll use it. The enemy took over radio, television, and the music world and while the world was staying in the dark ages, hoping it would go away, the enemy was busy making it happen. Over the time of my deliverance ministry, I have seen the enemy become more subtle. I have seen him modernize his business. **"Satan is definitely computerized and in cyberspace."** I believe the church and those of us in deliverance ministry need to update and modernize. We need to come into the real world and use whatever tools are available for us to reach people and see them delivered, using our full potential.

I want this book to stir ministry leaders. I want to say to them, "You need to wait a minute and take a look at things that are getting out of control. Also, you need to quit worrying about how you look as a leader and be more concerned about the actual situation." Church doesn't always look good to the world. You should just watch any talk show and see how Christians are portrayed. Listen to any Christian that has an opportunity to be a guest on one of these programs. They are kept down and not allowed to say a great deal about God. We are always talking about wanting to be like the early church. We are always talking about the early church movement and getting back to it. We need to understand that not all of what took place in the early church will work for us today. We can have the same success of the early church when we are not afraid to use the tools given to us to use by God. Instead of worrying about these things, we need to be using them.

## CHAPTER 13

## Training Leadership For Deliverance Ministry

There are sects, cults, and certain religious organizations that don't believe in electricity or driving cars. I am not condemning anyone choosing to live that way. It seems so many times these cults have the ability to get out of hand and in the process many are hurt. I don't believe this is what God wants to happen. So many times sex has been used by men to defile God's people. Sex was given to bring life into this world—to create life—also for pleasure between a man and a woman.

Things like computers are tools available for Christians to reach man. He said it in His Word, "That every knee shall bow and every tongue confess that Jesus Christ is Lord." For this to happen, the word must get out for people to begin to yield to Christ. The Word tells us to "Go out into the highways and byways and compel them to come in."

Compel is a deliverance word we need to understand. It means do whatever it takes to bring them in, for them to be delivered. If deliverance is to come to the church world, we have to use every tool that God has given us.

The devil has been smarter than the church because he has used whatever he needs to sell his message of the opposite traits of Christ. Where God is love, Satan's message is hate. Where God's message is unity, the enemy's message is division. Where God's people are righteous, Satan's people are un-righteous. Where we are holy, Satan is un-holy. Satan intends to counterfeit good for evil, it is always the opposite of God. So that's why I feel so passionate concerning deliverance and its place in the church to-day. So those people who were delivered will learn how to stay free of the demons and not let them back in. As a result, Satan will not receive the glory from what God has done in these lives. The degree of con-trol Satan gained over these people, includ-ing bodily movement and speech, will end. Some may require some follow-up work, some more intense than others.

Those in deliverance ministries must be

adequately trained to do this follow-up work, and most of those coming through this type of deliverance will need help. That's why a strong deliverance program is so badly needed. All those in leadership of positions need deliverance training for their ministry. And they need to have discernment to know if the demons are gone, or have returned. We can go on and "play" like the demons are not there. We must have leaders become aware of the need for follow-up and discernment concerning demonic activity, no matter how subtle, in whatever capacity it is in their ministry and for the anointing power to deal with these issues. I don't feel that we should allow the demonic forces to manifest themselves on the level that they have in times past.

We need to stop trying to defeat Satan on the same level that he is trying to defeat God's people. There is dunamis power. This is the same type of power that Satan is using. This is the power that, as we allow it, will gain strength, because it is like a dynamo. Look at how a hydroelectric system works—inside a dam there are large turbines and the more water allowed to flow through them, the faster they run and the more power they produce. We want to go beyond this power. There is exousia power. This power spoken of in the Word is the authority of the spoken word. When Christian men and women begin to travel in this authority and when you speak to the demonic forces, they will have to go to the place you send them. If you command them to the pits of hell, they'll have to go because we are using the authority backed by God and it is his Word that you are speaking. Men need to begin to use this type of anointing.

This anointing will not disturb the church. It is not something that will demean the church, but it is a place to start a building force. We begin to see individuals who have been tormented by demonic forces delivered. I believe that once this deliverance power is brought back to the church, leadership will see that a delivered person is more of a benefit to the kingdom than they were in their old condition. If the unforgiveness that keeps prayers from getting through is gone from the church, then nothing can be accomplished. If the hatred between family members is gone, can you image what the outcome could be? If anger is no longer a hindrance, not the righteous anger we have with the devil, it's the anger that we harbor at one another. Look at what has transpired recently in the world.

Robbers don't feel the need to wear masks because their intention is to kill. They are not killing for the money. They are killing because, to them, life has no value and they have a desire to take another life. What would happen if somewhere down the road deliverance was offered to these individuals? If they were raised in church, and the church had understood deliverance, they would not be where they are today, doing what the devil is directing them to do.

With a certain amount of discernment concerning deliverance, we can watch an individual's body movement, gestures, and speech. We are able to see the demonic forces that are in control of an individual's life. Most people will require intense follow-up after deliverance, and we need to teach leadership to know the different needs and levels of follow-up work. The tools used to help those with anger, bitterness, unforgiveness, and possible sexual perversion will not be the same as those who have been in the Satanist movement or in new age. The program for alcoholics, drug addicts, and homosexuality is always more intense. There is a need for programs geared to the depth or need of each separate deliverance. In all cases, follow-up work is absolutely necessary; some just more intense than others. Our goal is that once an individual is delivered, they are able to stay free and learn to trust the leadership of the Holy Spirit rather than leaning on familiar spirits that have been keeping them tied to the same behaviors.

The Holy Spirit showed that deliverance works that are more fruitful and glorifying to God are the deliverances where a person who loves God and belongs to Jesus becomes aware of the demonic strongholds in his or her life and desires to be free so the individual can be pleasing to God. They may not realize that these demonic strongholds are more oppressive than possessive and can sometimes be from outside a person. When we say outside, this could be like a temptation; most of the time the person is aware that trying to resist the temptation is more than they can handle. Although they are sincerely repenting, many times this sin comes back again and again. There needs to be a support program for them. They have a sense of something being wrong with them, but they don't know how to effectively find the answer. There are people in the church who are dealing with these problems. I am sure these individuals would love to be free. In this deliverance process, there has to be a way for the deliverance ministry to realize the needs of these individuals, and we must have sensitivity to their needs. These individuals cannot be delivered with a brazen attitude.

There are two demonic forces in the church that we need to be aware of: 1) where the enemy has manifested himself and you go after it; and 2) where the individuals are not aware of the problems in their lives. There is a sensitive way in which to teach these individuals how to be aware of their needs. Here's where the gift of discernment comes in. Because of our prayer life and the discernment we have, demons will reveal themselves in certain deliverance services. By being taught the deliverance process we can be aware of the demonic forces that people are not aware of. We know that these demonic forces are trying to hide. You need to have a way of going after these demonic forces. Matthew17:21 says, *"Howbeit this kind goeth not out but by prayer and fasting."* I believe this is the only way that the person can understand the deliverance process.

Also in counseling, Christian leadership must have the confidence of others. You know for a long time people believed "Deliverance" in the church name was just another word. If a church name said "Deliverance Tabernacle," it was just a name. We need to come to the place when we speak the word "Deliverance" we have an attribute ministry and we are able to fill the need of deliverance. The church has not been able to do it up to this point because it keeps denying that it is real. Denominations have convinced their people that demons are not real—but my friend, they are.

People have temptations or problems they want to overcome but have just not been unable to do anything about it. They have a sense that something is wrong but don't know how to effectively defeat the demons and the effect they have on their thoughts and feelings, causing them to be seduced into various sins and perversions.

Satan's motive is to embarrass the kingdom of God. He will use whomever he can and by any means he can. So God's people will be defeated and not victorious. Just look in the pews of churches today. There are many in church today, even in your congregation, that are living defeated lives. They are so discouraged by not being able to live a pro-ductive spiritual life. They give up, walking away from the church and God. Then they fill abandoned by God and those in the church. This is not what we want. Satan's intention, all along, was to destroy another

Christian.

Even after Christians come to God, they often still have some of these things buried deep inside that haven't been dealt with yet—things that have a strong grip on them. Maybe the individual wants help but does not know where to go to get it— because church has always been able to embarrass people. Deliverance ministry must come at a level that does not embarrass, degrade, or lessen an individual. A Christian should never be looked down upon or talked about, belittled, or made fun of. When someone comes to the church and says, "I'm having a problem and need help," we need to listen. Leaders should be fine-tuned in the deliverance ministry and ready to help those in need. New Christians should know that they are in a deliverance ministry and as problems arise, they can call the pastor or call whomever is in leadership and know they will discern and be able to help them with their problem.

Maybe you are dealing with lust and it keeps plaguing you. You should not be afraid to say so. Your pastor should have enough insight to say, "Come pray with me. We'll command that spirit to be gone."

Then you are given scripture to help you after you leave the church. There should be someone in the church who is trained to pray with you and be of assistance through this time until you are stronger and able to stand by yourself. Remember, that you are never alone. There should always be someone you can call if you have a problem.

We should institute a program with those that are trained in deliverance so when people come through deliverance there are people with wisdom from God to help them. Somebody who was a drug addict could take what they have learned to help bring others out. Talk about networking! Just imagine what could be accomplished by deliverance networking. The possibilities are endless.

I've learned in my deliverance practice that people who experienced a quieter and less showy deliverance are actually easier to bring through the deliverance process. It also helps that they have a very strong desire to be free from demonic influence. They really hate the sin that they have been grieving over for years. These particular individuals are more likely to hold onto their deliverance. When I command the demons to be quiet and not let them put on a show, they simply lose their hold, come out and go back to the very pits of hell where they came from. I believe that these deliverances are usually complete. Also, the Holy Spirit has shown that a more subtle demonstration is needed in the church today. We should not give the devil any glory. We should not allow the demons to spit, sputter, puke, or demonstrate; there are extreme cases that the devil just wants to come out without much work. In these instances, the devil usually gets more glory than he should.

I never will forget one case, just before I was to start a meeting, where a young woman was deep into witchcraft. She was a witch with costume and the ability to cast spells. She was good at her trade. Men at this particular church got her delivered. I started a meeting on Sunday night and about 15 minutes into it this young woman jumped down to the floor and began to jerk around. Her skirt rose above her knees and she began to bark like a dog. Men jumped out of their pews and held her down, commanding the devil to come out. She tried to bite them. They finally quieted her down. This happened again on the following Monday and Tuesday nights at about the same time, roughly 15 minutes into the meeting. I began to pray to God as to how I should handle the issue. On Wednesday night when the same thing happened, I told the men to remain in their seats. I looked the woman in the eyes and said, "In the name of Jesus, I command this devil to come out." The young woman got up off the floor, sat back down in her seat, and didn't utter another word. For the rest of the meetings she was intent on learning. As long as the enemy can get any kind of glory he will use every chance he can get. He knew the familiar spirits in this woman. I believe there is a place for this type of deliverance. We must take total authority immediately, when demonic forces are revealed in a service. Most Christians are not aware that demons are subject to us. The only power the enemy has is what we allow him to have. Demonic forces gain control over our lives because we give them the legal right to our lives. Demonic forces only get control in our lives when it is given. So we need to understand that we have the power and strength, not the devil.

Just think if Christians had stood up and protested, one individual could not have taken prayer out of school. It only happened because we allowed it to happen!

I don't mind if demons show up at my services, because I'm here to tell you that God is the only one receiving the glory for anything that happens there, as well as what happens in teaching leadership about deliverance through this book. Whatever is accomplished through this book is not to glorify Gary Ray, only the Lord. We must understand the need to take back whatever Satan has taken from us—our families, our children, and loved ones that have been ripped away. We need to take them back.

The reason this is not happening in churches is because Pastors, Leadership, and Administrators have a problem with deliverance. Maybe demonic activity is in their lives. When this happens, their ability to hear from God concerning the people's needs is hindered, distorted, and obscured. They truly believe they are doing their work. It's hard for them to believe that they have any problems. These individuals need a fresh revelation from the Holy Spirit. Some may need deliverance themselves. Through this book and the conferences, our desire is to make leaders more aware of their own situations.

We want leaders to realize that this is not a

put down, and our only desire is to see the church operating at full capacity. I know this is a broad statement and hard to believe there are still pastors and leaders who have uncovered demonic activity in their lives. It doesn't take much to cause problems—a blinding spirit or maybe a deafening spirit that prevents a leader from determining what is needed. Fresh revelations from the Holy Spirit need to be given to leaders of ministries; most of the time they never receive it. We need for them to receive the keys that will destroy the works of the devil, in their ministries, their people, and their own lives. This will require great sensitivity to the Holy Spirit and must be dealt with carefully. Our motive is not to destroy, but to build up leadership.

We know immediately what the enemy is going to try to sell to ministries. The enemy will convince some in the world to read this book just to see what it says, or to prove it wrong. Some will obtain my literature because others have given it to them. Some will take it and some will discard it. Our hope is that it touches lives. I know what the enemy is going to sell, especially to ministries and leadership, concerning this particular ministry. The first thought the enemy will put in their minds is that we are out to embarrass ministries. They need to know this is not the intent of this ministry. We want ministries to be built up. We do not want to embarrass pastors. Much of this work will be done, and no one will know it has been done.

I've been to many conferences where pastors could go to be strengthened, yet deliverance was never used to aid them. Pastors should be able to say, "I'm having trouble with my ministry." It should not embarrass a pastor to seek help. Ministries teaching deliverance as their main theme should make sure this happens. If leaders, administrators, teachers, and workers in a ministry need any form of deliverance, let us who understand deliverance see that those in need get the help. Then from this point we must teach these people how to help others. I guess you could call this type of deliverance "Multi-Level Teaching." We want to teach others how to live victorious lives, who will in turn teach others.

I know our ministry will certainly receive its share of abuse. The enemy will try to minimize it and cast a shadow of doubt over it. I say, "To God be the glory." First, it is not my ministry, it is God's ministry. We are not trying to destroy the body of

Christ, but build it up, because we think that the people we want to help are those whom God has called in the first place, as well as those Christians who want to live a demonic-free life. We want to help these individuals also. We want to teach the keys of deliverance to these people so they can destroy the works of the devil. We know that this requires great sensitivity through the Holy Spirit to be able to defeat these demonic forces.

I believe that some of these leaders will not participate in this. They may elect not to be a part because the idea of their people gaining unhindered communication with God and purity and power may threaten them. They may be afraid of their people being set free. They may feel that these people will in turn "show them up," or may gain spiritual superiority over them and they may lose control. Seeing the power and effectiveness may cause leadership to feel they are not doing their job, and it scares them. So they just allow the hindrances to continue. I will tell you this—the Holy Spirit said that this very subtle demon is the one that must be addressed now. The unsaved must see a reason to want what we have.

Sometimes I wonder if we ever think about what God's real intentions were regarding the death of Christ. We may have some idea, but let us take a closer look. First, what can God acquire through the total deliverance of the body of Christ? We know that the Word tells us that Christ came to be the second or last Adam. What was the reason for this? First we have to see who Adam was.

Who was Adam?

(Some people are especially remembered because they were the first to accomplish something. Neil Armstrong's name cannot be mentioned without thinking of the event for which he is most famous—he was the first moonwalker! Adam is to be remembered as Adam the first! He was the first in countless different ways, but he is especially to be remembered as the first in the following ways. Adam was the climax of the whole creative work of God. He was the image–bearer of God, his maker. The whole account leads up to the creation of humankind and there is then nothing else to be created.)[1]

He was the first man who God created from

the dust of the earth. The Word tells us that Adam had the very attributes of God, the very characteristics. In other words, when you saw Adam and saw how he walked and talked, you were seeing how God walked and talked. When God was ready to name the animals, he gave this responsibility to Adam. Adam didn't have to return to God and ask if he could call one animal "a dog," or another animal "a cat," because he had the Creative power—the very authority of God to do this (1 Corinthians 15:45-48).

We know Adam lost it in the garden because he allowed sin to enter. He could have stopped it, but he didn't—he allowed sin to enter. I believe had Adam not participated with Eve, sin would have been defeated there. Through the mercy of God, he sent his only begotten son to die on Calvary as the last Adam. His Son then gave us the possibility of having the relationship with God that the first Adam lost in the garden through sin—to be able to have His authority and nature.

The Word tells us this in Romans 3:22 (NLT): *"We are made right with God by placing our faith in Jesus Christ. And this is true for everyone who believes, no matter who we are."*

It is through Him that we are the righteousness of Christ, the hope of Glory. Just as the nature of God was in the first Adam, the same nature and characteristics are in us through Christ Jesus, the last Adam. This power and authority is ours if we choose to accept it. The enemy has been able to trip up mankind and keep it from accomplishing what it was meant to accomplish. Christ truly wanted us to have the power and the authority to administer the work. So we must accept this and do what needs to be done. We are to be these men and women of strength and power.

Through the Holy Spirit we have been given power and authority. I am not sure we realize all we have though Christ. I don't want us to continue being anemic Christians. I don't want us to continue to be weak and ineffective leaders. We must become powerful leaders, realizing the amount of power and authority Christ Jesus has given us. It is wonderful to realize what has been given to the body of Christ. Let us take it and begin to teach the rest of the body of Christ how to be free. This type of freedom, if we look in the Word, is to be reformed in his image so we can manifest the righteousness of Christ to mankind. The church has to be delivered and set free before we can set people free. Before we can make major inroads into the world, we must be delivered ourselves. We must be set free.

The church must be transformed into His image. Because the Word tells us that our words will not transform a life, but the example that we set is what is going to touch another life and cause it to be changed. So it is very important that we accomplish this now, because time is growing short.

We must get busy so we can see people delivered. Our hope is to see the final release of the church, which we believe is deliverance to come—so we can help others to reach their full potential through Christ. We want to see a new atmosphere and a new attitude in the Church world. Our hope is to create this. We desire to go deeper than ever before. There are other things that we would like to see happen. We need to make everyone aware that the Holy Spirit dwells in all of us for a purpose, so we can be beneficial to the body of Christ and able to help others. We must touch every individual who needs help.

"We need to shut the mouths of lions" is a saying that has been used frequently. There were times we would pray this way. We became aware, to shut the mouths of the lions, or to shut the mouths of those who don't want deliverance, we must become stronger than they are. So what they say will have no effect, and this will cause deliverance to happen in their lives. The only way we are going to become this type of individual is by becoming stronger than the lions. We must become more efficient than the unbelievers. Most people are defeated in deliverance ministries because they begin to think they have arrived. It is dangerous to think we know so much and assume the devil can't get to us, as we take pride and comfort in the knowledge we have acquired. At this point there is a place where the enemy is able to get through. This is an area we need to pursue a bit further. This is the area of intellect. The intellect becomes a playground for the enemy. One of the ways the enemy can get to us is through our intellect. We must watch out when we become healthy and guard against thinking we are untouchable. We become overconfident or cocky when we believe that enemy can't get to us.

In the area of a ministry of deliverance we must never allow ourselves to think that we know it all. There is a lot we can learn about the enemy and how he operates. Through teaching we can learn his process. We believe that through discipling—let's call it deliverance discipling—we can teach people and those in leadership how to become aware of the devil and his games. We must pray for anointing. Without the anointing we can't produce the real work of deliverance. There are people God wants to give the anointing to, and in the process they will need understanding. Within this understanding they will acquire knowledge to know how and when to use this anointing. We also want to put together a teaching series along with this book to help bring more awareness to the body. We don't assume we have all the answers. A hindrance in a strong deliverance ministry is leadership's inability to see the strength of the enemy—this is one of areas where we need to be teaching. I think that's something we need to be strongly aware of. For example, we don't always know the enemy, and this trips us up in our ability to win in this deliverance process. We must remember he is a subtle, shifty character. He comes in many colors and many flavors. He's sharp and knows the strings to pull and the buttons to push. We certainly need to be aware of this, especially on the leadership level.

We need to be able to see the strength of the enemy and not be fooled by him.

There was a subject that we talked about sometime back. Let us take another look at it. We may have already touched on some of this, but let us consider again the individual who comes into the ministry with a strong Jezebel spirit. This individual can be a woman with a strong hatred of male authority, and as before made a misjudgment over this malignancy that was growing in the ministry. With a problem like this (and this is to all leaders of ministries), all issues must be separated. Let me tell you what we have done as pastors. I'm talking based on the knowledge that I acquired as a pastor. We assume that what we have been doing will remove the problem from the church.

It is these Jezebel spirits causing the problems in our ministries. We assume that if we just get them out of the ministry, then everything will be okay. I can tell you it won't. You must kill the Jezebel spirit in the individual. This type of deliverance is strongly needed in ministries all over the world. We must directly confront these issues. We do not need to allow these malignancies to continue because they will con-

tinue to grow. We must deal with these spirits head on. We must never assume the
problem will go away by itself. Your people, whether they are women, men, or even
couples in the church, may not be happy
with what's going on. You may think by
getting them out of the church the problems
will go away. This is not true. The lions and
tigers are not what destroy the vine; it is the
little foxes, the people who are inside as
well as outside the church who will do the
damage. They will continue to hold their
influences over the ones they can. In these
cases we need to consider deliverance. One
time when we were pastoring there was a
spirit that came through town we were un-
sure of. We were not sure about the effect
on the church and the conflict it was causing. We believe a true move of God will not
cause conflict in other ministries, but this
one certainly was causing conflict. We
prayed to God at the time, "God, what's going on?" The Lord said in certain issues we
need to close our mouths and leave things
alone and allow these individuals to be
judged by the words they speak. Of course,
we definitely need to deal with things in
our ministries. In a deliverance ministry,
once we catch on to the process, we must
not use this as a tool to hurt other people or
ministries. Being uncertain about what was
going on, a friend and I asked for a meeting
with this pastor hosting the revival. Here

was another aspect of what was happening. At the time there were several other issues going on in our ministry that had put me into a weakened position. In a weakened condition we should never provide deliverance or even try to defeat the enemy. Before you do these things you need to get in touch with God. You need to make sure there are no problems in your own life. If there are things going on and you try to do deliverance, the enemy will pick up on it and he will use these issues to destroy any ability you might have to bring deliverance to this individual's life. We don't want to attempt to get on the devil's territory when we are in a weakened condition. The devil knows when we are fragile. This has happened many times, and it is very important that we don't do this. In teaching or instructing individuals, leaders, and pastors about deliverance, one of the instructions is to be aware of the blind side. Be aware of the areas that the enemy can get to. Sometimes we are looking in one area and we should be more aware of the devil's territory we are in, and then the enemy will not be able to blind side you. We know the one thing we should not do in deliverances is to go into the enemy's territory to do the deliverance unprepared. It's a lot better if you can draw the enemy to your ground. I've found that it's a lot easier for the deliverance process to take place if you get the enemy on consecrated ground. In other words, you need to get them into a place where the spirit of God is, instead of entering a honky-tonk and trying to deliver someone. If you can get the alcoholic into your territory, it's a lot easier to defeat the enemy. Don't be afraid of him because you're standing with God and the anointing. You need to be aware of this and not cower to the enemy, the devil. We want to make this point clear.

One other thing that we want to bring out is there is a spirit that has been going on from the beginning of time. It is one of the most prevalent "New Age" spirits we will deal with. It is called a Shaman. Let me share just a little bit about this spirit. I am not going to get too deep into this. Shamans are called witch doctors or medicine men. These were absolutely esteemed individuals in most tribes in Africa. Many Native American Indians were also shamans. The medicine man is the most respected individual in the tribe and is looked upon highly. We need to tell you this spirit is running rampant in the world today and looks very good. We must tell you that this spirit is making itself known even in established ministries. We need to watch and be aware of this New Age movement because it is infiltrating the established church, and this is a crack that the devil can get through. Some of these spirits will come out through prayer and fasting. God doesn't have to test you to know you because he knows you already. On the other hand, Satan will test you daily to see if he can win you over from God to his side. What I'm saying is we need to be strong in prayer and fasting to get to the level of deliverance we're talking about. This is what we want to teach the body of Christ. We want men, women, and leadership to be aware of this enemy so it can't blind side us—so this New Age spirit cannot infect the body of Christ anymore and we can see what God has intended to take place, we can see it manifest itself.

God knows who you are already so God doesn't have to test you to find that out. He will, however, use things to point you to events that have already happened in your life. God does not do bad things to good people to get their attention. He does not have to. He already knows who you are, but the enemy will test you to try to draw you away from God and get you to question God. This is his way of getting you on his side. We must be aware that he will do this, especially in a deliverance ministry. The enemy will try every trick of the trade to keep you from getting individuals delivered. You always need to be aware of this. When problems or situations arrive in your ministry, you must always look for the enemy's footprint or signature. There will always be something to let you know where the enemy is. Whatever demonic force is in your life, it will always show itself. You must first realize "pride" is not a Godly virtue, but is certainly a virtue of the enemy. A demon cannot stay hidden forever; he may lay dormant for a time, but because of the pride in him he must reveal himself. I've had individuals come through the deliverance ministry who had been molested. In one particular case a woman in her early teens had been molested, and at that time a demonic spirit was able to impregnate her—even though she loved God, was saved, and was a member of the church and still seeking God. Here's why deliverance is so important— because nobody ever dealt with this situation before. This spirit lay dormant and did not reveal itself until this woman was thirty-four years old, married, and with a family. The spirit began to manifest itself, and it was uncontrollable at this point. At this time even the church was unable to deal with the problem.

The church didn't even recognize the problem until one night in a service the discernment came and the demonic spirit was revealed and deliverance took place. This brings to light that the issue can be a demonic force and lie dormant for many years and later reveal itself, even after a person is saved. I had an individual come through my ministry that had been molested by her father. She thought she was all right, but then later in her life she began to have problems and found it hard to sleep. She was making decisions and doing certain things that she would never have done on her own. She was under the influence of the enemy who was causing the problems. Through deliverance she's healthy today and able to function. We need to be aware of what the enemy can do and how he can lay dormant. Yet, there is a time when the enemy must raise his head because of his pride. We need to be aware that this demonic force can lay dormant for years and that it will always reveal its true nature.

This could be what we are seeing beginning to happen in the church world today. This demon force has had a grip on ministries and churches for years. I'm not sure if this is a real word, but I love to call this a demon of religiosity. There is a definite difference between a religious and a demonic spirit, and you can know the difference. At this point what I am seeing is a dormant church. I see churches that have a sense of security, and yet are at risk. I see a spirit of religion taking control of many churches, and they are in trouble. We are at rest in Zion, unaware of what is going on. Death is just around the corner. What is happening is the church is being drawn deeper and deeper into the grips of this religious spirit.

The demon is able, at this point, to send his little imps into the church and give you a false sense of security in the place where you should feel the safest. The church should be the safest place for an individual to be.

The Word of God says in 1st Corinthians 3:16: *"Know ye not that ye are the temple of God and that the spirit of God dwelleth in you."* We need to realize that <u>we</u> are the church, not the building. The building is just rock and mortar, steel, and aluminum. Strike a match and the building is gone. But our bodies are the temple of the Lord. I'm talking about the church as a whole, the as-sembling of people together. The fact that he is able to send demonic forces into the church and give us a false sense of security in the place where we should feel the safest is frightening. I do believe there is an awakening going on in the body of Christ.

It's happening now, through this ministry and many other ministries of deliverance who want to teach and instruct and bring people to the awareness of what's going on within the body of Christ and the need for deliverance. There is an awakening in the church of the delivering spirit. Some of these demonic spirits have lay dormant in the church for years but are now being revealed to the body of Christ. I'm not the only one who realizes the need for deliverance. In talking with other ministries, I find other ministers and pastors are becoming more aware of the need for deliverance. They are beginning to see these spirits being revealed within the walls of their own ministries. These spirits have been inside the church. The spirit of religiosity has been in the church for years. It has been fueled in some instances by denominations based on the fact that men have gained control over ministries and have initiated their own ideals and beliefs. They gain control over what God wants. God never wanted men to control the people. I learned this in my pastoring. In my heart of hearts I wanted to do something. When I went to Florida to begin my ministry there, my heartfelt intention was to bring these people out of where they were at the time and give them something they had never had before—to bring them to a level where they had never been before. That was my desire, and I assumed that if I could get control over their lives, I could do just that. I'm going to tell you something—that's not what God wants. God does not want us to control people; however, we need to be in control with God of our ministries. We see the leadership of a lot of denominations pushing their theories, not God's, on the people. You know that God, even though he is in control of your life, does not control you. You have the right to make your own choices. It is free will with God, and yet he is in control of your life if you allow him to be. I think we need to be aware of this. We do not need to be controlling but to be in control of what's going on.

I believe many things are beginning to be revealed, and we're starting to see that there are those we assume to be saints, but they are not. Someone needs to reveal them or at least make the church aware of them. Of course, there again, this needs to be taught to leadership. These demon forces could be defeated through leadership with the knowledge. I want to assure you of one thing. This will never be done by a novice or someone that is a babe. Deliverance should never be done through these individuals. Leadership needs to be taught today so they can also teach others. I am hopeful we eventually can accomplish this.

My prayer is to see this happen. I am aware of what the Word of God says about this. Let us quickly look in the Bible to the Book of Mark regarding the events unfolding after Christ's transfiguration on the mountain. He came down from the mountain and there was a great multitude about him. The people came to him and were greatly amazed and he asked the scribes a question. Ye were them? There was a man in the crowd who answered. Of course we know the story about the young boy who had the dumb spirit. Several people, as well as some of the disciples, tried to get the young man delivered, but they were unsuccessful. Then the father told Jesus what the problem was and what was happening. Sometimes the spirit in him would cast him into the fire or the waters to destroy him.

He says in the latter part of verse 22 of the 9th chapter of Mark, *"If thou canst do anything have compassion on us and help us."* And Jesus answered in verse 23, *"If thou canst believe, all things are possible to him that believeth."* Now out of that statement the father of the child cried out, *"Lord, I believe, help thou mine unbelief."* And Jesus healed the boy, immediately. Then in the 29th verse of the same chapter, at the end, after he had done this, he said unto them, *"This kind can come forth by nothing but prayer and fasting."* So, there's a level of things that happen and we must have a consecrated life. Listen, what it is going to take to accomplish this consecrated life is to be willing to give it all to the Lord. If we can see this happen in the church, then we can begin to reach the world with this message of deliverance. We can begin to see these young children tormented and hurting and being defeated daily by the devil, and we can begin to see it destroyed in their lives.

It is sad to see what is being perpetrated on our young people today. They are being bombarded in the schools with such issues as homosexuality, and now they are initiating this teaching in schools—the concept that homosexuality is an alternative lifestyle and not a bad thing. I'm going to tell you it is a bad thing. It is a demonic spirit and we've allowed it to get into our schools. It started the day we allowed one person to get prayer out of school. If we, as a Christian nation, would have stood together we could have defeated that. Now we have a situation that is going to be difficult to defeat. That is why I am so adamant about teaching deliverance. We need to see men and women delivered. There are Christians today that are fighting for this first amendment right, the right of free speech. I want to give you something to think about, concerning this first amendment right business. No matter what decision is made in the natural, it will always affect someone else's first amendment right. The lawyers can fight until the cows come home, but every time a decision is made in the natural, it will affect someone else's first amendment right. There is not a way to administer first amendment rights. Here is an example. If we make a decision to put prayer back in school, it will affect the rights of those who don't want to pray. If we take prayer out of schools, then we infringe on the rights of those who want to pray. The only way to administer properly is through Christ Jesus. Tell me there doesn't need to be a strong deliverance ministry in every church. When one individual can effectually change a biblical principle, tell me the enemy doesn't have strength and there is not a need for deliverance. You're not going to tell that to me. So, you know, we need to be aware of what the enemy has planned to transpire. As preachers we need to look in the mirror and see the face looking back at us. I just think that we need to step back as ministers—and when I say ministers I'm talking to the complete body of Christ because everyone has a ministry of some kind. Whether it is a call to preach, teach, or to be of the ministry of helps, we all have a responsibility. Every individual in the church has a ministry.

Let's go one step further—to pastors and leadership. We've got to become aware of this. Tell me that there's not a need of deliverance in the body of Christ—when individuals are sitting in churches and one family is sitting on one side of the church and another family is sitting on another side of the church and they hate one another and can't get along—always in competition with one another. Don't tell me that we don't need deliverance in the body of Christ, and let me tell you what deliverance will begin in the house of God. If there is a need for healing in the church, it will come through the body of Christ. Regardless of how you perceive the end time work, we need to make any inroads into what is going on in society today—no matter how you see Christ coming again—no matter when you believe He's going to come back. Eschatology beliefs have nothing to do with what we're talking about here. His son will come back. Like He said, He'd come back. He's going to do it the exact way He said He would, but if our mind is simply caught up on the issue, then we have missed it all. We are told in His Word to occupy until he comes back.

Don't think for one minute that you can just sit on the bench or the sidelines doing nothing, thinking everything will be alright, just waiting on him to come back. This is the wrong answer. **"You can't be delivered from something unless you are being delivered to something."** What did I say back at the beginning of this book? **A delivered mind will create a new direction in a person's life.** Listen, we need a new direction.

**HELLO**, here I am preaching again. Please understand that what I'm saying is so very important. Listen, we can't reach mankind, or initiate change, when we're trying to do it on the same level as the enemy. Using the same process the devil uses will not work. We must take the authority.

As stated early on, there are two powers that we would utilize in being with what we can use and what the enemy uses. The first is "Dunamis" power. This is the power that reproduces itself. It is like the dynamos we see in the large dams—the more water you force through them the more power they produce. This is the kind of power we have against the enemy. The second power is known as "Exousia" power. This is the power which gives us the ability to speak with power and authority. And this is the power in which the enemy is able to operate in.

We need to quit being naïve. We need to realize that we will not defeat the devil trying to use the same process that he uses. We are a step above. We should be a head above anything the enemy is attempting. He's a thief. Stealing is his nature; it's all he knows. God produces life, Satan can't produce life. He can only give death. We need to realize what is going on. Listen, we need to operate with His authority and take back the territory the enemy has stolen from us. Whatever territory the enemy has acquired, we gave it to him. The Word of God informs us that the enemy has told us this is the devil's territory. I tell you it isn't. God said that this earth and everything in it belongs to Him. Whatever the enemy has, he has stolen. Now is the time for us to take it back using the ministry of deliverance. We allowed it to creep into the body of Christ, and we've also let it separate and divide us. We need to come together now, not just in unison, but in true unity. We are beginning to see deliverance in our lives, and we are teaching deliverance to others. This can only bring strength back into the body of Christ. I believe if he said "occupy till he comes," he doesn't mean to occupy in weakness. He means to occupy with power and with authority. Always in deliverance we need to be selective in dealing with demonic forces, using only the power and authority of the Holy Ghost. We don't need to try and take on the world; we need to deal with one issue at a time. We need to begin our deliverance ministries with one group at a time. When there is a door open we need to be teaching the message of deliverance. We need to be selective through the Holy Ghost by setting aside time, never walking blindly. Another thing we need to do is always seek the direction of the Holy Spirit. Why do we say this? Well, there's a scripture that gripped me a long time ago, and it's a scripture that we use. It's found in 1 Corinthians 2: "Here are some things that need to be revealed to prepare us." In Verse 9 it states: "that as it is written eyes have not have not seen nor ears heard nor either has it entered into the heart of man the things which God has prepared for them that love him."

The problem is we never go any further than that. Here is what we would like to teach people. In Versus 10 through 12 it says, "But God has revealed them unto us by his spirit, for the spirit searches all things, yea the deep things of God." Now we have received not the spirit of the world but the spirit who gives from God, that we might know the things that have been freely given to us by God. Understand what God is saying here. We have been raised in the church thinking that we have not seen nor heard, neither has it entered into the heart of man the things which God has prepared for them that love him. Then we stop there and stir up the body of Christ—thinking Wow! There will be a day when we'll understand. Listen, the Word of God says in Verse 10 that God has revealed them unto us. **How**? By his spirit. Verse 12 says, "Now we have received not the spirit of the world but the spirit which is of God. That we might know the things that are freely given to us of God." We do not need to limit our ability. Stop thinking that someday we'll know all these things. God is revealing it to those who are now filled with the spirit. This is what this ministry is all about. But we want to make the body of Christ aware of what we can accomplish. We can't just sit around waiting for Him to come back and take us out of this mess. Because, you know, Eye has not seen, Ear has not heard, neither has it entered into heart of man what God has prepared. The next verse tells us that it's not through the message of men, but only by the spirit— because the spirit searches the deep things of God. It's the spirit that gives us direction. It's the spirit that gives us the knowledge. The one thing we need to understand is that we are able to see by the spirit. We need to operate not by the spirit of man but by the spirit of God, through the knowledge of the Holy Spirit. We need to learn to travel by the spirit, not by what knowledge we've acquired.

The thing that I realized is when I left Florida, I left because I was mainly relying on only my personal my feelings at that time, rather than stopping and listening to what God was saying. We must learn to move based on what the spirit is saying, not by what we are feeling. We must always travel by the spirit.

Demonic forces are not defeated by our years in the ministry or by our knowledge. Hear what I'm saying. What we are trying to get across to leadership through this ministry is that the demonic forces we're after will never be defeated by our years or our knowledge or the number of colleges we've attended. Never mind the number of degrees hung on our walls or how many times we've read the Bible this year. The forces will not be defeated by that; they will only be defeated by the spirit—by allowing the anointing to come upon us in a way that we can lay aside everything that has the ability to beset us or put us aside, or get our minds off of the real issues. The enemy is good at deception. There are great lessons yet to be learned, if we will listen to what God is saying in our lives.

A committed, yielded life is what it will take to get the job done. The average week-end Christian cannot accomplish these kinds of feats for God; he or she must be trained. I know this is hard to understand, and it may be all right for you to just say that I am an old sinner saved by grace. Actually, no, I certainly was saved by grace, but I'm not an old sinner. I'm not a sinner any longer. What I am trying to do here is to make you understand that we're supposed to be productive while we're here. We need to understand that we are the righteousness of Christ, the hope of glory. Whatever happens and whatever benefit Christ has in this world he has it through you. He says I have this in earthen vessels and you are that vessel. You have to understand that if the work is done, it will be done through you. If it is accomplished, it will be accomplished by you. I don't want to hurt your feelings, but God isn't going to do it for you. He said, "I will do it through you," not for you. We're sitting and waiting for God to defeat the enemy in our churches, and the enemy is running wildly because if the enemy is defeated, it will be

through us. God said that there is the promised land that belongs to you, but you will
have to take it. How can you accomplish
this? He said that everywhere the soles of
your feet touch, it is yours. Does that tell
you anything? People, we need to get to
work. We need to get busy. You need to understand that just being a 'get-by' Christian,
a weekend Christian, and/or a Christian
who goes to church on Sunday morning is
not what will defeat the enemy. We must
lead a consecrated, committed life. We
must be yielded to the process. Sometimes
it's very difficult to understand what exact
effect this will have. The Lord tells us to do
our first works over again. Sometimes this
is a hard process—even sometimes regarding the number of times we have to do
them. It hurts, it hurts, it hurts. To me, this
is probably the most important part of everything that I've put out to this point. These
are important issues. We can no longer
maintain this anemic status and still be able
to accomplish the task at hand. Men and
women, it's time. We need to quit fighting.
I'll touch on an issue very sensitively. We
need to quit fighting for control.

One of the first issues that needs to be addressed in every ministry is the Jezebel
spirit. This thing that has been sold to the
church is called, **"Women's Rights."** The

Bible gives everybody rights, but when we begin to single them out, we get into trouble. The Bible tells us what the position of a man is, and what the position of a woman is. We need to quit battling one another and just begin to fulfill the responsibility that is given to us in the Word of God. We will then begin to see an effective church. When people ask this question concerning what men should do in the church and what women should do in the church, the Word tells us. The enemy is there to accomplish one thing and that is to create separation. Divide and conquer. If the enemy finds a crack and he can come through and create any separation, he will defeat us and cause us to not accomplish what God has intended for us to accomplish. We need to see this. We need to quit subscribing to this thing. Women, be women. Be proud to be a woman. Don't try to assume a male role. Men, quit fighting. If you'll take your position in the church that was given to you by God, there won't be any problems. This issue will be eradicated and no longer will the enemy be able to come in and destroy churches with Jezebel spirits. Stop laying all the responsibility on the women. Understand, there are male dominant spirits that are at work in the church trying to erode what the women's role is in the church and trying to undermine it, belittle it, and demean it. That's not what God intended.

Now, maybe we shouldn't deal with this issue in **deliverance**. I think we need to know what our place is. Christians are sitting on the pews of churches all over the world. They are not being effective because they don't know what their role is. There are so many different thoughts and theories out there. We need to take a firm stand on what the Word of God says. If we operate based on what the Word of God says, we'll not lose. We'll be the winners. If this deliverance message is allowed to go forth the way that it should, we won't be the losers, we'll be the winners in the end—if everyone begins to take a rightful position—if we'll just begin to show the character and the nature of God. Let us understand that when Jesus walked this earth He did mighty things; there's no question about that. After the cross, after the grave, and when He came back He tried to make those people aware he couldn't stay here and be beneficial. He could only affect those that He could minister to. If He went away, then He could send the third person of the God head, the Holy Spirit, so that He might live in us. So, as a disciple of Christ in the day that Jesus was on the earth, he couldn't live inside me because he was in the flesh. I could only learn from him when he was there.

Since the Holy Spirit was sent, He is now able to live in me all the time. It says the Holy Spirit will dwell in you and live in you. Many Pentecostal people think that the Holy Spirit only comes when we sing choruses like, "Come Holy Spirit I need you." The Holy Spirit should be living in you daily—so that Christ could be seen daily and he could be with us all the time, and he could teach us daily. Who is this person, "The Holy Spirit" that dwells in us? Who is He really? It's the character and the nature of Christ. The character and nature of Christ dwelling in us is a beautiful thing. This is what I'm trying to create through this ministry—I'm trying to teach leaders how to get back to that place where we could be men and women of authority. We want to stress that we are able to speak to the demonic forces because we are learning how to recognize the enemy. There are many leaders and pastors that just don't know what's going on in their church. Why? Because they aren't able to recognize the trick of the enemy. Oh, there are big things that the devil does that we could see. The world is bad. It's not that we aren't to be concerned about this. Yes, we ought to be concerned about the world, but the greater need is for us to first clean up our own front porch. Understand that we aren't going to be able to effectively change the world until we can change the environment around us.

Here is another place where deliverance is needed. There are so many churches that began because people became emotionally excited after a meeting and wanted to start a church. They began drawing people, especially those who couldn't get their way in other churches. The one thing we do not realize is that these people that could not get along in other churches simply bring their problems to this new ministry. After a while these churches begin to diminish and people begin to scatter. Why? Because in the beginning they got people who were unhappy and looking for something new. Of course, these are people who travel. These are what we like to call spiritual gypsies. They go from one place to another looking for the emotional moment until someone holds them to the line and expects them to do something, to commit. Believe me—I understand the process because I've been there. These gypsies love to stay as long as they feel the emotion, but when they have to get to work or actually comment or submit, they run. If a ministry cannot evangelize the area that it is in (with people drawn from the local streets and town), it will never be effective. There has to be a deliverance. There has to be a process that takes place and it needs to manifest itself strongly. It needs to happen now, to-day. There needs to be a strong deliverance in the body of Christ. We will never effectively change the world until we effectively change the place that we're at. We'll never evangelize the world until we evangelize the neighborhood where our ministry sits. We need to understand this and we need to understand it fast.

Let me tell you about a particular survey question: "Are gay rights a threat to the American family and its values?" This was a poll taken from Christians, not the world. This was asked of members of the church. The results showed that 45% said yes and 51% said no. Does that tell you something? Does that tell you where the church is?— when Christians say, "well, they have a right too; God loves everyone so we must love them too"? The homosexuals' way of promoting themselves to the established church is by saying that the New Testament teaches that God is love. Sure, God is love. He loves the sinner and hates the sin. He will not accept sin under any circumstance. We've got men and women sitting on the pews of our churches today whom we know have problems in their lives. We need to address the issue. That's what this teaching is about. It's what we're trying to bring to pass. We need to realize that we can set many (not all) churches free—if we can just get men and women delivered from these things that have grip upon their lives. They just need deliverance from excess baggage they are carrying. This must occur before anything else can happen. Then we can begin to seize an opportunity—beginning to go out and take the territory. "Occupy, Occupy." The scripture is given to us in Luke 19:13, *"and he called ten servants and delivered them ten pounds and said unto them, occupy till I come."* Have we not heard this all our lives? Occupation is nine-tenths of the law. I believe we need to be busy about the Father's business. We should be less concerned on how big our ministries can be built. It has to be about reaching one person at a time, seeing to it that they are delivered. I would encourage every pastor and every director of a ministry go through their membership and to begin to ask God to give them the discernment, and give them the anointing with deliverance power, going one on one to the individuals taking care of their problems. I believe in the beginning when you approach the problem, the individual may be taken aback for a moment. If we, as ministers, are traveling under the anointing of the Holy Spirit with the discernment given by God, we are asking God to give us the discernment to recognize the enemy, to recognize the demonic force. Pastors, study the different kinds of demon spirits that there are. Learn them. Learn what their traits are. Learn what they do. Learn what an addictive spirit can do. Learn how an angry spirit acts. Know what someone on alcohol looks like. Learn the tell-tale signs of the individual on prescription drugs. Learn what the signs are of people that are depressed and under stress. As leaders, we must know this. We must know what's going on in people's lives. We need to quit assuming that the problem is outside the church and realize that the problem is in the church. The devil already owns the sinners—those outside the church. He is now trying to get to your people, and he's using subtle measures to do it. We, as ministers, are so busy doing other things that we don't realize what the devil is doing.

I think we need to be very careful in deliverance sessions, making sure we are following the dictates of the Holy Spirit. We believe that one of the main ingredients in anyone whom is in a deliverance ministry is the need to have a proven track record with others of their ministries. They need to have the power of discernment and cannot invent methods that satisfy their fleshly wants and desires. They have to totally and completely move with discernment and operate within the perimeters of the wishes of the Holy Spirit or God. It is very important that we don't invent measures or plans of our own. We must have a spirit of discernment to know what God wants to be accomplished. This same discernment level will allow us to be able to find the demons that need to be cast out. Then we also need to learn that, in some cases, some problems can be resolved through extensive counseling by people who are trained in this area. It is not always necessary to have a long drawn-out deliverance session—this only allows the devil to gain too much territory. So I think these are issues that definitely need to be addressed in any reliable deliverance program. If these programs operate that way, then we know it is not a hocuspocus ministry. We don't need to remove demons from individuals using the same processes or coming up with the same gimmicks the enemy used to get these individuals to take these demons inside in the first place. So it is very important that we watch what we do very closely. Our desire is to get people delivered, not to impress other people with our ability, knowing that if we do this we are always allowing the enemy to gain more strength in these individual's lives.

We must remember that our main objective is to see individuals totally and completely delivered and able to work freely for God.

## About the Author

Gary Ray has been in full time ministry since the 1980's. He himself experienced a miraculous deliverance from drugs after having a career driving some of the most famous rock bands around the country on tour. God had greater plans for Gary's life and set him free from a $1500 a week cocaine addiction. Since then Gary has continued to help others become set free from addictions and demonic spirits that would do nothing but steal, kill and destroy their lives.

Gary has ministered in the U.S., Canada, Jamaica, Puerto Rico, and Nigeria. He has literally seen it all and witnessed God's power in setting people all over the world free. He took it a step further and became a Certified Temperate Counselor and earned a BA in Christian Counseling.

Today, Gary still travels with his wife Ophelia sharing his testimony of deliverance and speaking on the subject to whoever needs to hear that God is still in the delivering business.

Gary currently lives in Nashville, TN and has two daughters, Tiffany and Valerie and a son, Dustin who reside in TN as well.

## To Learn More About Gary Ray or Schedule a Speaking Engagement:

gary@garyraymin.com

www.garyraymin.com

## To Order More Copies or Inquire About Group Discounts Contact:

info@garyraymin.com

## Other Materials by Gary Ray:

Gary Ray Tours Again DVD

www.ingramcontent.com/pod-product-compliance
Lightning Source LLC
Chambersburg PA
CBHW052104090426
42741CB00009B/1665